WHEN
WE
PRAY
TOGETHER

Emilio Castro

WHEN WE PRAY TOGETHER

Risk *BOOK SERIES*

WCC Publications, Geneva

Cover design: Rob Lucas

ISBN 2-8254-0953-7

© 1989 WCC Publications, World Council of Churches,
150 route de Ferney, 1211 Geneva 2, Switzerland

No. 40 in the Risk book series

Printed in Switzerland

Table of contents

Almighty God,
here we offer unto Thee our thanksgiving and praise,
that Thou hast brought us to this hour
and this act in the faith of Christ
and by the power of the Holy Spirit.
As Thou hast prospered those
into whose labours we enter,
so, we pray Thee, prosper us
in this our undertaking
by Thy most gracious favour,
that in all our works
begun, continued and ended in Thee
we may set forth Thy glory,
for the well-being of Thy Holy Church
and the salvation of all Thy people.

Prayer by Archbishop of Canterbury Geoffrey Fisher
following the unanimous vote that constituted the
World Council of Churches
at its First Assembly in Amsterdam, 23 August 1948

1. The Ecumenical Significance of Prayer

At the front of the main assembly hall in the Ecumenical Centre in Geneva is a large mural that depicts Christ and the churches around the world. Its inscription reads, in Greek: "That they may all be one".

The words come from the 17th chapter of John's Gospel, which records Jesus' "high priestly prayer" during his last meal with the disciples before he was crucified. It is an appropriate caption for this painting, because those six words from Jesus' prayer are the permanent point of reference for the ecumenical movement.

As we confront the present reality of divided churches and the persistent difficulties of overcoming centuries of separation, Christians are called back again and again to that prayer of Jesus. It is a source of consolation, for if our Lord prayed for the unity of his church, then church unity is surely a possibility. It is a source of strength, for in taking this petition on our lips, we acknowledge that it is only in the company of Jesus that we can continue to pray and to work — *ora et labora,* as the motto of the Benedictine order says — for the unity of his church.

Prayer is the very heart of our being in the ecumenical movement. Without prayer we would have given up the search for the unity of the church in discouragement long ago.

This is not to say that this quest has been without results. On the contrary. The progress made towards church unity in this century, particularly in the forty years since the founding of the World Council of Churches, is a cause for deep gratitude. Today, for example, with Roman Catholic participation a common feature of ecumenical encounters, some may be surprised to learn that at the First Assembly of the WCC in Amsterdam in 1948, not a single one of the Roman Catholics invited was allowed by church authorities to participate. While the Roman Catholic Church is not yet a member of the WCC, our collaboration is growing and irreversible.

The Roman Catholic Church is only the most visible case of transformed attitudes in relation to other churches. Similar accounts could be given of rapprochement between Reformed and Lutherans, between Anglicans and Orthodox, and so on.

But as Jesus' prayer "that they may all be one" gives us a measure of ecumenical progress, it also fires us with impatience over the shortcomings of our ecumenical initiatives and the slowness of our ecumenical journey.

To be sure, in today's pluralist world not all Christians consider the existence of so many denominations as a scandal. Living in fiercely competitive societies — especially in the West, but increasingly in the rest of the world as well — we may be tempted to explain this multiplicity of churches as just one more manifestation of the spirit of the age.

But those who have caught the ecumenical vision "that they may all be one" cannot accept this status quo. We cannot sacralize our present divisions, because we have heard and prayed the prayer of Jesus, which calls us back to our vocation and gives us the courage to continue.

Because prayer is central to the ecumenical movement, no ecumenical encounter takes place without an opening moment of liturgical celebration and common prayer. Ecumenical newcomers, exposed to the World Council of Churches for the first time, often profess astonishment (and sometimes impatience) that, instead of plunging immediately into the consideration of serious global problems, we take time to be quiet, to listen to the Bible and attune ourselves to the Christian tradition, in order to receive inspiration for our work.

Unity in God's self

"That they may all be one" is no mere slogan or proof-text. Nor is it without significance that these words are taken from a prayer. When we read them in their context in the gospel, we see how Jesus sets the unity of the disciples — and thus of the church through the centuries — in terms of God's self. "I do not pray for these only," he says, "but also for those who believe in me through their word, that they may all be one; *even as thou, Father, art in me, and I in thee,* that they also may be in us, so that the world may believe that thou hast sent me."

From this prayer it is evident that the primary motive of church unity is not efficiency of organization or maximizing of influence. Jesus' prayer sets the unity of the church in the framework of believers' relation to God; even more, he sets it in the framework of the eternal relationships within the life of the Triune God. The Son, in conversation with the Father and in the love of the Spirit, takes the unity of the church upon himself as a particular concern, hope, expectation, *prayer*.

It was important for those first disciples, who were being trained in the spiritual life by their ministry of prayer with Jesus, to realize that Christian unity — among themselves and down through the generations to come — is one of the most intimate aspects of our relation with God.

Not only does Jesus' prayer at this point in his life provide an *example* to those first disciples who were with him around the table and to those who have followed him in the generations and centuries to our own day. It is also an *encouragement* to them and to us. Even if differences appear, even if fear overcomes us, even if we are scattered, even if ignorance and misunderstanding and different ways of looking at things tend to separate us, it remains forever true that the Son, with the Father in the power of the Spirit, has prayed for the unity of the Christian family. We cannot go back.

On our ecumenical pilgrimage, whenever we feel disheartened by the obstacles to be overcome and the disunity that remains in the life of the churches, this reminder that the unity of the church is not our human cause but is God's own cause is fundamental.

Jesus' petition for the unity of his followers in this prayer before his death on the cross is a permanent reminder for Christians today of the importance of praying for the unity of the church. Praying for unity should be a normal feature of church life in every local parish. Church unity may never be relegated to the status of a hobby for a few specialists. It belongs to the sharing of the gospel: it means sharing in the concern of God's very self.

But Jesus' words not only provide encouragement and a model: "even as thou, Father, art in me, and I in thee". He also speaks of this unity in God's self as the content and reality, the centre and heart, of the unity of the church: "that they also may be one in us".

The ecumenical enterprise, in other words, is a search for the unity of Christians *in* God's self. As we come closer to God in prayer, led by the Spirit, we inevitably come closer to each other. Overflowing grace embraces God's people into the reality of eternal love in the Trinity. Bringing us into the mystery and richness of love, it asks us to show in everyday life the reality of our belonging in God. Our unity is a participation in the internal unity of God's self.

When we describe church unity as Jesus prayed for it in such trinitarian terms, we are reminded of the freedom of operation in the Trinity. The three persons have their vocations, but these are worked out in an eternal constructive relationship, a common will for the salvation of the whole of creation.

There are moments of tension when the Son does not understand the will of the Father, as in his prayer at Gethsemane to "let this cup pass" and in his cry on the cross: "My God, my God, why have you forsaken me?" But that question, even dissent, arises within the reality of a common purpose and assurance that as the drama evolves the whole will be seen as fulfilling the original purpose of redemption.

Likewise, the unity of the church, conceived in the model of the Trinity, is not something uniform or monotonous or conflict-free. We grow together as churches within a permanent dialogue of give and take into the reality of our being in God.

The WCC, in its Fifth Assembly in Nairobi (1973), described this relationship as "conciliar fellowship". Although the English expression cannot fully convey the meaning of the Greek *koinonia* — of belonging to a spiritual reality in which we embrace each other in the same embrace by which God takes hold of us — "conciliar fellowship" highlights the fact of recognizing the other as my partner, my *alter ego,* the one with whom I am together in a common discipline and reciprocal commitment.

So this prayer of Jesus both describes the dynamic of spiritual growth that brings us together and provides a model in which the diversity and the unity bring us together into the mystery of belonging-in-God, and into the dynamic of the Trinity, which is finally the all-embracing spiritual reality.

Praying for mission

The prayer of Jesus links together the unity of the church with its mission in the world: "that they may all be one... *that the world may believe"*.

Understanding mission as being sent on behalf of God, the ecumenical movement, whether in everyday programmatic activities or in public statements or in meetings and conferences or in visits with churches, encourages the church to that priestly role which is its fundamental vocation.

We must remember that this mission is always local. To be sure, missionaries may go from one community or country to another. But they cross frontiers in order to be incorporated into the building up of the body of Christ in a particular place. So, too, our prayer should incorporate the totality of the life and mission of the churches in every country of the world.

We pray for the gospel to be proclaimed to those who have not yet had the chance to come to know Jesus Christ. We pray that as people encounter the story of Jesus Christ, the Holy Spirit will illuminate the encounter and enable them not only to understand that story but to embrace it and commit themselves to discipleship of Jesus Christ.

This evangelical dimension should be a permanent feature of our prayer, in order to avoid selfishness in our Christian life. If we keep our Christianity to ourselves, we are claiming a right to possess something that belongs to our neighbour. God has sent the Son to illuminate, to deliver, to save the whole world, not just to preserve the few Christians.

Our prayers for the mission of the church will include petitions for sisters and brothers and children working in sectors of society other than our own, whether in our country or elsewhere in the world. The classic prayers for missionaries who have gone abroad are naturally a part of our ecumenical prayer as well, but always with care that we do not elevate prayer for our dearest ones — which is legitimate and indeed necessary — from our intercessions for those with whom they are working and for the community into which they are being incorporated. Ecumenical prayer for mission is finally a prayer that the gospel will actually be proclaimed in many communities and that many people will come to a personal, living encounter with it.

Too often our "prayer for missionaries" overshadows our prayer for the churches where they go to work. We attach more importance to what our sisters and brothers and children are doing in this or that place than to what the Holy Spirit is already doing there. We must be reminded that our understandable pride at seeing our daughters and sons incorporated into the work of the family of God somewhere else should be complemented by a sense of humility about our and their place in the vast scheme of God's plan.

A more serious flaw that may arise in our prayer for mission is that our sinfulness and cultural limitations may lead us to confuse the missionary being of the church with a certain sense of Christian superiority over against people of other religious convictions. Sometimes a factional or proselytizing or even imperialistic tendency gets smuggled into our prayer for mission. In our zeal to see others encounter Jesus Christ, we may come very close to identifying mission as the worldwide expansion of the influence of our own church institution — or even of our country.

In our prayer for mission we must keep before us the awareness that God's love is already present with those to whom we are sent, and that they, too, are objects of the care of the Holy Spirit. So we pray that the missionaries of the church may carry out the task of witness to the name of Jesus Christ in such a way that this testimony will illuminate the total human experience of those who hear without destroying those values which the Spirit of God has already helped to create in their lives and experience.

When we pray together

What are we doing when we pray together ecumenically? Obviously, ecumenical prayer, like all genuine prayer, begins in a humbling of oneself before God. Together, we try to raise our contemplation to God's self. In that sense our personalities and identities are relegated to a secondary level of attention and importance.

Of course, God wants each of us as the person he or she is called to be. We are not copies of each other: everyone is a mysterious, single creation, a masterwork of God's wisdom. But when we come before God ecumenically, our eyes go out from ourselves towards the wonderful presence of God's grace and splendour. In so doing we are immediately invited to surrender, to offer our differences, including our confessional diversity and all the differences which it produces, in the presence of that higher reality of God's love which embraces us all.

So the first consequence of praying together is a humbling of ourselves in order to recognize our very being in God and thus, having contemplated our different identities in the light of a higher and the only divine identity, God himself, a better ability to look back at ourselves and at each other.

Secondly, by praying together ecumenically we are already making public our commitment to search together for that for which we are asking God. How can we pray for God to pour out love in our hearts if we are not willing to offer the best of ourselves in love to our neighbour? How can we be honest in our prayer if we do not immediately, with whatever means we have at our disposal, attune our will, our very being, to the response to our prayer?

By being together in prayer, we are already embracing each other, already showing that love which is the prerequisite for the growth into the being of God which is the final reality of Christian unity.

One could also make this point in more mundane terms. As we come together to pray for unity, it is almost impossible not to discover things we can do in common. We create sociological and psychological bonds — shared convictions, friendships — that keep us together to face the realities of the day.

The ecumenical movement is not yet at the point at which every church feels free to participate in the eucharist offered in every other church. Moreover, the World Council of Churches stated explicitly very early in its life that a church's participation in the WCC does not necessarily imply that it recognizes all other member churches as real churches according to its own ecclesiological criteria.

Yet as we have grown together in prayer and worship, in acts of witness and service, we have in fact come to recognize each other. *De facto,* we already accept one another as churches. What we need is to strengthen our intellectual capacity so that we can articulate consistent doctrinal formulas that do justice to the reality to which our praying together has already attested.

In discussions with Roman Catholics it is often said that in the ecumenical movement the churches have a degree of communion which, although not complete, is already real enough to allow us to give a common witness. The fact that we can pray together across confessional, cultural and national differences is one indicator of this. We should not underestimate what a fantastic reality this is. I would go so far as to say that at the moment we come to prayer together, our communion *is* complete, *is* perfect, because it is communion in God. It is not merely communion among Christians, but a common encounter in the reality of God.

We come back to the text with which we began: "that they may all be one; even as thou, Father, art in me, and I in thee, that they may also be in us". The secret of the unity for which we pray is the unity with Christ in God, the unity of our belonging to the mystery of being listened to and being provoked in prayer by God. At that moment the reality of communion, the reality of church unity begins. What is lacking is the description of that reality in words that would enable us to overcome the doctrinal and ecclesiological barriers that still separate us.

Of course, the ecumenical movement is an encounter not only of different traditions, loyalties and theological perspectives, but also of diverse types of spirituality and devotion. This diversity can be enriching and inspiring; but it can also raise obstacles to our praying together, unless we can enter into those differences in a way that enables us to understand what fundamental Christian values are being manifested and promoted by styles of prayer that are foreign to us.

Let me make this more specific by reference to my own background as a Latin American Methodist. As a small minority in its part of the world, my tradition was characterized by a certain overreaction against the classical liturgical style of the Roman Catholic Church, to which the overwhelming majority of the people in Latin America belong.

In my tradition it was taken for granted that extemporaneous prayer is the only proper form of prayer. We defended extemporaneous prayer vigorously, arguing that in order really to open up your heart before God you must find your own words or your own sounds. We were very critical of other traditions, especially the Roman Catholics who read or recited prayers from many centuries ago.

But in the ecumenical dialogue we began to realize that our prayers were not quite so extemporaneous as we had imagined. On the contrary, they tended to become more and more a repetition of phrases which had never been written down but had become sacralized into what was at best a tradition (even if we didn't call it that) and at worst a cliché. Much of our extemporaneous prayer was no less mechanical and automatic than what seemed to us to be thoughtless repetitions of the Our Father or the rosary or the creed, which we criticized so sharply in other Christian traditions.

Moreover, when I began to experience ecumenically the worship life of Orthodox and Anglicans and Lutherans, it was a shock to hear Scripture lessons chanted. I had a hard time understanding what possible benefit there could be in adorning the simple reading of the Bible in this unfamiliar way.

Again, however, I gradually began to realize that what had happened to the reading of the Bible in my church — and to my own reading of the Bible. All sense of mystery had been lost. We affirmed dogmatically that the Bible is the Word of God, but we handled the Bible in a cavalier spirit, without trembling when we opened it.

And thus, when I see the series of prayers and the parade of priests and deacons and children and choirs bringing forward the gospel to be read in an Orthodox liturgical service, I might still wonder if they are not perhaps sacralizing the Book. But at the same time I recognize that they are calling the attention of the gathered community to the fact that something very important is going to happen when that gospel is read.

My tradition allows for an easy, direct access to the Scripture. But perhaps my tradition has not been able to surround and undergird that open Scripture with the worshipful prayer for the coming of the Spirit that is absolutely necessary to illumine its pages and to provide the sense of sacredness coming from it. So ecumenically I needed to go through the exercise of understanding what the others were trying to do.

Of course, as I hear the corrections of their spirituality to mine — not so much explicit as coming through their very being — I hope they are also listening to the corrections that come from my tradition to them.

I hope that they too are coming to appreciate the need to incorporate into their ancient liturgy an awareness of contemporary tragedies and hopes, so that these awesomely beautiful services are complemented with prayers that speak to the realities of today, and this fiercely preserved tradition does not become a protective wall but rather a doorway for flesh-and-blood commitment and witness in our world.

I hope, too, that the veneration of the Bible so richly manifested in that liturgical tradition is accompanied by a pastoral presentation of the message of the Bible that will help people to go beyond an awareness of the mystery of the Word of God to an awareness of its challenges for our daily life.

One area of difference that may be an obstacle to praying together ecumenically arises from different understandings in various traditions of the role of the saints and of the Virgin Mary in our intercessions.

When we come together ecumenically as Christians from differing confessions, we sometimes celebrate liturgies from the respective churches. Those liturgies may commemorate the names of the saints or of the Virgin Mary, remembering their lives as realities that form part of the context of our prayer to God — pointers to the fact that the communion of saints is not only *spatial*, covering the whole inhabited earth, but also *temporal*, stretching backward in time and forward to the Lord's return. It is not so much a demand for intercession by the saints as a presence that is invited and acknowledged.

Of course the basic text for this practice comes from the ancient ecumenical creeds of the church: we believe in the communion of the saints. Our communion with each other and our love for each other also incorporates the love of the generations that have gone before us into the presence of God, and as we intercede for each other in this life we are also supported by the intercession of those who are already in the blessed company of God.

In some local Roman Catholic devotional practice, direct appeals are made to a particular saint or to Mary through the name given by the sanctuary where a particular apparition of the Virgin is celebrated. Popular devotion, accepted by the church, even makes what we might call a certain division of labour among the saints. The Vatican sometimes declares this or that saint to be the patron of this or that profession or this or that nation.

As a Protestant I have many personal reservations about these practices and this "division of labour". But I do not want to speak too quickly, because I realize that for the masses of poor people in Latin America some of these devotions, which seem to me to verge on superstition, are the "earthen vessels" inside which the possibility of listening to the gospel of Jesus Christ is incorporated. We should be careful, as we call on each other in ecumenical discussions to purify our practices and expressions, not to throw away the baby with the bathwater.

Let me try, as a Methodist, to suggest a theological and spiritual undergirding for this practice, which confessionally is not my own, but which some of my fellow-Christians bring to the ecumenical forum. Can this practice be a source not only of polemics and division but also of mutual challenge and inspiration? Can it invite and provoke me to go more deeply into my own prayer life?

In Christ humanity has been forever incorporated in God. Whoever loves God in Christ loves his or her brother and sister. In that experience of loving, even to the point of losing one's life, one is loving in the neighbour the Christ who has made his own that neighbour's destiny. Thus, although the immediacy of my relation with God cannot be broken by any kind of intermediary, my neighbour is not an intermediary, but is the one in whom the immediacy of God is being perceived, for in the life of my neighbour I am loving God.

If it is true that God in Christ has made the destiny of reality his forever, the kind of human relationships we call horizontal are never really such. They are always sacramental relations, in which we perceive the reality of God. So prayer which remembers those who were blessings of God in our life and in the life of humanity and in the history of the church, prayer which recalls the faithfulness of Mary the Mother of Jesus, is one way to recognize this intimacy of relation with neighbours in God and with God in neighbours. It is one way of feeling that we belong to the centuries and to receive from that realization the courage to be and the courage to pass on our faith to the coming generations, because God from all eternity takes care of every one of his children.

Prayer is not a selfish exercise between my soul and God. Prayer is the moment at which I am a priest to my neighbours in the whole of humanity. In Jesus Christ, the only real priest, all of our concerns are taken into the mystery of God, which by grace embraces not only the militant but also the triumphant church.

The Week of Prayer for Christian Unity

The Week of Prayer for Christian Unity, which antedates the founding of the WCC by almost a generation, is probably the best-known of the various organized instruments for ecumenical prayer.

By the late 19th century, a concern for Christian unity was manifesting itself in almost every Christian tradition. Among the significant pioneering events and initiatives which grew into the modern ecumenical movement, besides the Edinburgh missionary conference in 1910 and the encyclical letter of the Ecumenical Patriarchate of Constantinople in 1920, are the movements of prayer for the unity of the church, especially those associated with the names of Paul Wattson in the first decade of this century and of Abbé Couturier in the 1930s.

For more than twenty years now, the international preparation of standard materials for the Week of Prayer for Christian Unity has been jointly undertaken by the World Council of Churches and the Roman Catholic Church. A delegation of each body meets annually to review and revise prayer and Bible study materials which have been prepared by a local ecumenical group somewhere in the world. So we might say that the Week of Prayer is a symbol of growing church unity even before it actually takes place.

What this joint preparation brings to the Week of Prayer for Christian Unity is the dimension of official commitment by the churches. The spiritual concerns which the Week of Prayer had from the beginning remain, but on a much wider geographical scale and with a much more serious church commitment to participate, to open up their internal life to the presence of others and together to pray for the unity we search for all year long.

The hope, of course, is that this growth in both numbers and in level of commitment is something that matters not just once a year, but comes to visible fruition in these churches' ongoing concern for each other and for the unity of the church.

What do we pray for when our congregations join together locally to mark this Week of Prayer? Behind one of the historical precursors of the Week of Prayer for Christian Unity — the Octave of Christian Unity — lay Paul Wattson's hope and prayerful expectation that all Christians would return to the Roman Catholic Church. Abbé Couturier was — if we may put it this way — less specific. His oft-quoted phrase was a petition for "the unity of the church of Jesus Christ as he wills and when he wills".

Few people today would understand the first of these two formulations as the goal of the Week of Prayer for Christian Unity — or of other ecumenical activity for that matter. But I am somewhat uncomfortable with the second formulation as well — not because I do not believe that the unity of the church will come about "in God's time", but because I fear that this kind of "eschatological" perspective on church unity too often brings with it a sort of fatalistic lack of urgency and passion.

To see church unity in an eschatological perspective, I believe, does not mean relegating it to "the end of time", but being aware that the last times, the coming of Jesus, impinge on our present reality and call us to change our ways. As we see especially in some of Jesus' parables, eschatology is a permanent attitude of being ready for the final surprise, for the coming of the bridegroom, so that we prepare ourselves for that encounter.

Yet, we should not be too critical of these theological expressions of how and why Christians of an earlier day began to pray in an organized way for church unity. Not surprisingly, these expressions reflect their values and their limitation to a particular worldview and ecclesiastical perspective, which we are not necessarily obliged to share in order to be heirs of their passion for the unity for which Christ himself prayed.

Let us be honest. Consciously or unconsciously, all of us bring some ecclesiological perspectives and convictions to our prayer for church unity. While I do pray for the unity of the church in the mystery of the Trinity, I do so as a Protestant, more particularly a Methodist. It will be difficult for me as I pray completely to banish from my mind any notion of what a church united in the trinitarian mystery might look like on earth. Everyone who prays for church unity does so with a "model of unity" in view — whether of an exclusively "spiritual" unity of the church or of a "super-church" with powerful institutional machinery or anything else in between.

But in our prayer for church unity, as in all of our prayers, we recall Jesus' promise: "whatever you ask the Father *in my name* he will grant". In other words, the name of Jesus is a kind of filter that controls and purifies the limited and sinful content of our prayer.

We obviously pray with our whole being in the company of people who have the same passionate commitment to this or that historical cause or historical perspective. But finally we need to be humble enough to deposit that prayer before God with the awareness that by itself it is unworthy to be received; and we ask for it to be purified from the perspective of Jesus.

I believe that those ecumenical pioneers who prayed for the unity of the church expecting that it would correspond to the model they had in mind — which we, no doubt unconsciously, do as well — would have been humble enough to submit this understanding of church unity to correction in the company of the faithful.

The aim of the Week of Prayer for Christian Unity is to bring to the consciousness of the churches and to the experience of their members once a year the visibility of the unity we already have and the awareness of our call to be one, and then, as a family of God, to introduce before God the tragedy of our division and to plead for inspiration and power to overcome those divisions.

Of course, local congregations — no matter how much inspiration they may have — lack the power or authority to overcome many of the historical divisions between churches. Disagreements about eucharist, for example, are discussed in national and international theological dialogues; doing something about the division caused by these disagreements is largely beyond the possibility of the local group. Still, the local prayer for Christian unity can create a ferment, a gentle (or not-so-gentle) pressure on church authorities to move with more speed and urgency along the path towards unity.

Moreover, the Week of Prayer is an occasion to discern those things which can be done together locally. In many places concrete projects of service to society and common witness to the gospel have emerged from the dynamic of the Week of Prayer for Christian Unity.

One such place is Istanbul, headquarters of the Eastern Orthodox Ecumenical Patriarchate of Constantinople. Christians form a tiny minority in Muslim Turkey. Unhappily, their small numbers have been confessionally divided through the centuries. Not only are the classical Catholic, Protestant and Orthodox divisions present; there are also many sectors of Orthodox churches which accept the authority of Rome, but have a certain autonomy — almost like separate denominations — within the Catholic family.

The fact that, in the context of the Week of Prayer for Christian Unity, these minority churches can meet each other and visibly recognize each other as belonging to the same family of faith, despite centuries of division, is notable in itself. But it also has consequences for the climate of relations among Christians for the rest of the year.

The instrument of local ecumenism in Istanbul, the Clergy Group, came into being to organize the Week of Prayer for Christian Unity. From there they went on to develop other common activities during the rest of the year.

To be sure, we should not romanticize the Week of Prayer for Christian Unity. In some localities it is more like a diplomatic tea party or homage grudgingly rendered to church leaders — be they in Rome or Geneva or at denominational headquarters — than a deep spiritual outpouring of the passion to follow Christ's will and way. There are too many places where nothing about the celebration of the Week of Prayer for Christian Unity in a local setting · affects any change whatsoever in the climate among the churches.

That is a sad reality which we need to confront and to challenge. At the same time, it is not the whole story. Even where a congregation that is not at all ecumenically minded takes part in the Week of Prayer for Christian Unity out of a sense of obligation to denominational headquarters, its coming together with others at least provides a chance for mutual encounter and perhaps for discovery that the caricatures people and churches have of each other miss the mark.

Moreover, since prayer is the opening of our life to a relationship with God which we cannot control, even a prayer that begins as the routine fulfillment of a mandate decided on elsewhere has the chance to become the centre of a renewal or of a new vision with consequences for the local situation. Prayer is always an expression of hope. And the Week of Prayer for

Christian Unity should be an expression of hope for Christian unity.

Of course, the Week of Prayer does not have a monopoly on prayer for the unity of the church or Christians praying together. There are also weeks of prayer organized by the Evangelical Alliance or the YMCA and days of prayer organized by various other groups in the churches.

In Latin America — the region of the world from which I come — the majority of the non-Catholic churches do not belong to the ecumenical family of the World Council of Churches. The Week of Prayer for Christian Unity is not familiar to many Latin American Christians; and although it is making inroads, it is not yet a high point of the Latin American ecumenical year. One could easily cite examples in Latin America of participation in the Week of Prayer as a routine and unenthusiastic fulfillment of requests coming from abroad. Perhaps this is because the Latin temperament is not so regularly fixed to specific celebrations.

At the same time, one can point to exciting examples of genuine rediscovery, in prayer together across divided church families in Latin America, of the symbolic nature of our being together the whole year around — for example, in facing human rights violations in Chile. And out of this externally induced obligation to be together something ecumenically good may come into being.

The ongoing life of Basic Ecclesial Communities and continuing Christian collaboration in defence of human rights are permeated with prayer which is not necessarily related to a specific occasion in the year. The vibrant togetherness of Christians in El Salvador, Nicaragua or Brazil is not linked to a church calendar but to everyday life situations that demand a commitment which cannot be offered apart from common prayer.

Along with the Week of Prayer for Christian Unity, the annual day of prayer in March, which began over a century ago as an initiative of women in the United States is having an increasing impact worldwide. Unfortunately, the churches have often looked at that initiative from a certain patronizing distance, as a good work organized by courageous women, but not something to be officially encouraged, facilitated or stimulated.

Even today when we list examples of ecumenical collaboration, including the Week of Prayer for Christian Unity, we often overlook this day of prayer initiated by women. Perhaps the leadership of our churches finds it difficult to accept the importance of something organized not by church authorities, but by voluntary lay movements within the church. In that, of course, we are totally wrong, because the church is precisely the *people of God*. Wherever initiatives like this arise, which invite people to pray, in relation not to their confessional identities but to their common affirmation of faith in God as manifested in Jesus Christ, and which evidence a search for the leading of the Spirit in the challenges of today, churches should recognize the manifestation of the freedom of the Spirit of God, which contributes to the total richness of the church.

The World Council of Churches is itself the fruit of many such movements. The laity movements, the Student Christian Movement, the YMCA and YWCA — all of these were in existence before the WCC and they contributed to creating a climate and providing leadership for the Council.

So we need to recognize that the prayer of people, official or unofficial, but organized with the same concern for overcoming our confessional divisions in the presence of the Lord and bringing to him the needs of the world and our anxiety for the unity of the church, is central to the life of the ecumenical movement. We would not be able to do without it.

Fortunately we do not control the Holy Spirit, who surprises us again and again — within official ecumenical structures or by creating new ecumenical structures, but also entirely apart from any ecumenical structures whatever — calling God's people together in prayer, Bible study and committed action.

Glory to thee, O Lord, Glory to thee!

Heavenly King, Comforter, Spirit of truth,
Who art everywhere present and fillest all things,
Treasury of all good and giver of life,
Come and dwell within us;
Cleanse us from all unrighteousness,
And of thy goodness, save our souls.

Daily Office, Orthodox

2. Some Varieties of Ecumenical Prayer

No doubt the first thing that comes to mind when we discuss praying together in the ecumenical movement is prayers of intercession. This is surely as it should be: as a conciliar movement, a fellowship of solidarity walking together into unity, we need to discover and support each other. What better way to grow into such unity than bearing one another's burdens, first of all by "taking them to the Lord in prayer", as the old hymn puts it?

The Ecumenical Prayer Cycle

Recognizing the importance of interceding specifically for the needs of individual churches as they seek, often in contexts of hardship and suffering, to live faithfully to their gospel calling, the WCC publishes an Ecumenical Prayer Cycle.

As its name makes clear, it is the vocation of the WCC to be a *world* movement. And the best word to describe the worldwide nature of the ecumenical movement is "solidarity". In the solidarity that comes from belonging to the global ecumenical family, churches in the most diverse situations — whether confronting the temptations of power or the challenges of powerlessness, whether facing widespread alienation and secularism or struggling daily to survive against totalitarian ideologies — find the strength, inspiration and courage to resist and the capacity to give and to receive.

In order to grasp the reality of this worldwide fellowship, made up of such diverse churches, we are driven to the deepest level of what it is to be a community of faith, that is to prayer and worship, to the contemplation, adoration and supplication of God.

The Ecumenical Prayer Cycle is a concrete attempt to foster the growth of this already existing reality. It provides brief information about the life of the churches in every nation and a schedule by which Christians in every part of the world can pray for those in a single geographical area during the same week. The Ecumenical Prayer Cycle is both a fruit of our being a family of solidarity and an instrument to root that solidarity ever more deeply into the life of faith, to increase that solidarity by the awareness of the other and to enable us to fulfill our priestly role of interceding one for another.

In the very process of producing and revising the Ecumenical Prayer Cycle we have been confronted with political problems

— not just in the descriptions of the countries for which prayers are requested but even sometimes in the name of a given country or the question of whether a particular geographical area should be listed as an independent country or as part of another. We have not tried to smooth out the rough edges of these unhappy realities: the fact is that situations of political conflict in the world also intrude into our prayer life, where they appear as challenges to be faced and opportunities for bridgebuilding.

In this way the Ecumenical Prayer Cycle is a symbol of the wider ecumenical reality. At its best it will serve as a resource, a pointer in the right direction, calling for imaginative use by congregations, small groups on retreat, youth camps and other local gatherings of Christians — as well as individuals who want to enrich their personal prayer life.

Of course, our petitions of intercession for and solidarity with churches in a given part of the world are by no means the only element of a full prayer life. Our own personal relationship with God, our immediate family, our local community, areas of crisis in the world — all of these, too, must be addressed in our daily prayers, and these cannot be included in a global calendar such as the Ecumenical Prayer Cycle.

Furthermore, we recognize that many individual churches produce daily or weekly devotional materials which suggest prayers and Bible readings for their members. Indeed, in some churches a daily liturgical celebration in the local parish is an essential part of life. We are grateful for the availability of such aids to spirituality, and we do not intend the Ecumenical Prayer Cycle to compete with or replace the spiritual disciplines for which churches are already providing resources. But we hope that its potential for complementing these existing materials will be of increasing help to the churches everywhere as they seek to realize what it is to be part of a worldwide family of Christians and to exercise their priestly vocation in growing solidarity.

Intercession does not replace other forms of prayer, but it is at the heart of the Christian life. That is the burden of the apostle's words: "You are a chosen race, *a royal priesthood,* a holy nation, God's own people" (1 Peter 2:9). This priestly calling is of the essence of Christianity. The Christian is placed between God and the rest of creation, as a priestly servant, caring for the whole of reality. The church becomes a place of intercession for the entire world.

Shorn of this intercessory dimension, our prayers can easily fall victim to our own selfishness. It is a tragedy, I think, that in many (if not most) Christian liturgical celebrations we spend more time praying for ourselves and the often petty concerns of our daily lives than in addressing the struggles and fears and hopes of the *oikoumene,* the whole inhabited earth.

As we look in this chapter at some of the other aspects of ecumenical prayer, it is in the context of affirming the basic importance of intercession.

Openness to God

What do we do when we pray together ecumenically? Ecumenical prayer, of course, shares many of the characteristics of Christian prayer in general.

The central reality of any Christian prayer, whether by an individual or in a small prayer group or in a congregational worship service or in an ecumenical assembly, is the opening to God of the totality of their being by those who are praying.

Philosophers and theologians and mystics have used a variety of language to describe this attitude of contemplation of God. They speak of a search for a depth-dimension in reality, a deeper awareness and meaning than we can observe or control in our mundane day-to-day existence. From the human side, prayer is an internal disposition to be quiet and open to the perception of a mystery that is revealed, a deeper reality which becomes a close reality, a perception of standing over against the Totally Other who has, in the person of Jesus Christ, become the Totally Near.

The person at prayer is not engaged in a monologue. He or she expects to be listened to, to be addressed as well as to address. But we perceive this hoped-for reality, pointing towards dimensions that escape our rational analysis, through the psychological limitations of our human existence.

In any kind of prayer, individual or collective, this openness brings with it vulnerability to alienation, to self-deception or even self-hypnosis, to manipulation of the very being of the person praying through techniques that are developed by himself or herself or practised on him or her by others. Then, instead of being tuned in to this world of deeper reality we have been speaking about, one escapes into a world of fantasy.

Prayer has the potential of being the most beautiful moment of human existence. Just as works of art may open up to us a dimension of reality that goes beyond the limitations of our rationality, so through prayer we escape from those rational restrictions. But Christian prayer must always seek this transcendence without evading the real world of conflict and human realities.

That means we as Christians must be extremely humble when we defend our practice of prayer. We therefore make our prayers in the name of Christ, not just as a liturgical formula but as an acknowledgement that we pray in the contemplation of the person of Jesus Christ, in the memory of his life. Here lies the importance of what Jesus said to his disciples: when the promised Holy Spirit comes (and it is the Holy Spirit who awakens us to the potential of prayer) it will be to remind them of all Jesus had taught (John 14:26).

And so in our prayers, as we open ourselves up to the contemplation of a reality we do not control, we are helping to give flesh and blood to that reality by the contemplation and remembrance of Jesus Christ.

This opening to the search for God in the permanent remembrance of Jesus Christ is precisely what distinguishes Christian prayer from other manifestations of prayer and from numerous other exercises in meditation or self-control or self-development (which may in themselves be extremely worthwhile and helpful for Christians as well).

As we open our selves to God in Christian prayer, we do so with our total being. As we pray we cannot cast aside all those aspects of our life which belong inherently to it. The contemplation of prayer is not a mystical experience isolated from our existence in the world and in history.

The Old Testament Psalter illustrates this. The Psalms are a tremendous school of prayer. In many of them the poet brings the contemplation of nature into prayer. The examples are familiar: "When I look at thy heavens, the work of thy fingers, the moon and the stars which thou hast established..." (Psalm 8:3); "The heavens are telling the glory of God; and the firmament proclaims his handiwork" (Psalm 19:1); "The Lord is my shepherd, I shall not want; he makes me lie down in green pastures. He leads me beside still waters" (Psalm 23:1-2); and supremely Psalm 104 — which is a kind of creation account in the form of a hymn of praise.

Throughout this contemplation of nature and creation, the Psalmist is issuing an invitation to worship God, who is the same active God in history as in nature.

This is not mere aesthetic contemplation. Aesthetics is transformed into prayer when the awareness of beauty is united with the awareness of action, of power, of the manifestation of God's liberating will. The Psalmist's contemplation of nature in prayer is in effect a contemplation that goes *behind* nature to the God who has been active in the Exodus and the history of the people of Israel and who continues to be active in the life of all creation. Contemplation for the Psalmist is the mystique that brings to the awareness of the mystery of God in creation the conviction that the same power active there will be active in the life of his people.

Confession and gratitude

What follows immediately upon this contemplation of God in Christian prayer is quite naturally the recognition of our sin and an opening before God of our awareness of our own shortcomings and limitations. Contemplating the presence and activity of God in the history of the people and the history of Jesus Christ awakens in us a realization of how far we are from being worthy of entering into communion with such a magnitude of truth, love and redemptive concern. In the life of prayer, awareness of sin is always a consequence of the contemplation of God.

The young Isaiah in the temple gives vivid expression to this: "Woe is me! For I am lost; for I am a man of unclean lips, and I dwell in the midst of a people of unclean lips; for my eyes have seen the King, the Lord of hosts!" (Isaiah 6:5).

A similar perception dawns on the younger son in Jesus' parable recorded in Luke 15. When he "comes to himself" and decides to go back to his father, he prepares his own plan of salvation: "I will arise and go to my father, and I will say to him, 'Father, I have sinned against heaven and before you; I am no longer worthy to be called your son; treat me as one of your hired servants'" (Luke 15:18-19). He has the solution to his problem. But it is only when he is embraced by the love of his father that he realizes the full seriousness of his predicament. He no longer has any plan, only the recognition, "I have sinned", and the expectation of the merciful judgement of the father.

Genuine confession of sin, unmasking our being and stripping away layers of self-justification to expose the reality of our being, is possible only within the prayerful contemplation of God. But when that repentance happens in Christian prayer, it leads us into life, not death. It is a repentance that takes place within the awareness of God's mercy, of which we are unworthy but thankful recipients.

Needless to say, even in the act of confessing our sins we remain sinful. And a persistent temptation of ecumenical prayer, particularly in the context of intercessions for those who are victims of injustice and oppression around the world, is a readiness to confess the sins of others. We shall return to this problem later.

Out of this recognition and acknowledgement of sin, our prayer becomes an expression of gratitude. Often people express their realization of blessings received in manifestations of joy that take the form of a veritable explosion of emotion. In its deeper meaning, this is an expression of gratitude to the underlying power of a universe in which such blessing or demonstration of love is possible.

Perhaps we in the ecumenical movement do not often enough remember in our prayers to express gratitude for the reality of the unity of the church which is already visible. For those who are active (especially as staff members) in ecumenical organizations, the programmatic details of working together and the frustration at the obstacles we still encounter may divert our attention from how much "real though imperfect communion" we have already received through God's grace. Needless to say, this sense of ecumenical gratitude will be accompanied by a renewed commitment to the unfinished ecumenical task.

The balance between gratitude to God and self-satisfaction over against my neighbour, however, is a delicate one. I cannot be genuinely thankful to God for the health granted to me or my children without at that very moment realizing how many other children of God are not beneficiaries of the well-being for which I am giving thanks. As a prayerful awareness that God has acted in a token way in a particular moment of personal or collective history, Christian gratitude inevitably asks "But what of the others? Why have they not received these tokens of God's favour?" And thus our response of gratitude leads us back to our vocation of intercession.

I cannot separate my gratitude for gifts received from my responsibility to ask for gifts in relation to those in the community around me who continue to suffer. I marvel when I see persons with mental or physical handicaps who can raise prayers of gratitude to God for the gifts they have received — love, joy, moments that have tremendous meaning for them. It shames me to see how they are able for the moment to accept the limitations of their handicap and become fully immersed in contemplating the blessings of God. But obviously I cannot enjoy my healthy state unrelated to a sense of solidarity with those who suffer — a solidarity that grows into an anguished prayer: *Why? What of the others?*

So Christian gratitude, which is the normal and fundamental expression of our spiritual life, is always linked to assuming responsibility to intercede on behalf of those who are victims of conditions that have somehow been overcome in our own case.

Furthermore, our prayer, as a complete opening of our whole life to the total reality of God, cannot avoid bringing our protests, our rage, our fight against God at the reality of a world which is so out of harmony with God's intention for his creation as we perceive it in Jesus Christ.

Our prayer today tends to be too delicate, too controlled. We seem fearful of disturbing God, and so our prayer takes the form of a sort of middle-class exercise in good manners. No matter how bad things are, we keep a stiff upper lip.

Against that background, it is surprising to read the bitter protests against God recorded in the Bible. Job is the paradigm of this type of prayer, which does not accept easy answers but fights until the contemplation of God provides not the intellectual solution he wanted but an awareness that God is still alive and that, notwithstanding realities we can neither accept nor control, there is a mystery revealed in the experience of prayer which gives manna for today and hope for tomorrow.

This is the experience of Jacob wrestling with the angel. It is the story of Jesus, praying in Gethsemane "let this cup pass from me" and on the cross "my God, my God, why have you forsaken me?" Unless our prayers give evidence of such protest and struggle with God out of the depth of our very being, something is lacking in their seriousness.

This is what makes ecumenical prayer so vital and so difficult. At the World Council of Churches we sometimes receive protests from Christians about liturgical materials we have sent out for use on special days of prayer for victims of severe injustice or suffering in a particular region of the world. These people say they cannot make their own the prayers which have been formulated by Christians in places like Chile or South Africa or Namibia, expressing in highly emotional terms their impatience with the prevailing injustice from which they suffer or even asking God to overthrow an oppressive government.

It is not surprising that these ecumenical prayers are difficult to receive in a different context, insulated from the bitter realities out of which they emerge. At the same time, these prayers powerfully remind us that the biblical tradition of struggling with God for answers to our human anguish continues to be vital and present in the life of our Christian family.

Theologically, perhaps, these prayers are not as pure as they should be. When I take their words onto my lips in the comfort of the beautiful city of Geneva, it may seem a bit tasteless. We need to see them as cries of despair — but cries of despair before God, who is the one who takes the reality of protest and transforms it into an awareness of hope, courage to resist, power to survive.

All of these elements of our prayer — contemplation, recognition of sins, gratitude, intercession, protest — are offered in the name of Jesus Christ. All of them focus our eyes on the life, death and resurrection of the one who has shown us such a life of dedication to others, such a totality of surrender to God, such a spirit of forgiving love, such a liberating redemption that he is worthy and willing to screen the prayers we address to his Father.

Even in prayer we do not trust in ourselves. We do not presume on our piety. We do not consider that our prayers earn us merits before God. We surrender our very being in openness to the being of God. And in the spirit of Jesus Christ we await the purification — not only in the age to come but in this age — of our desires and expectations.

Liturgical prayers: structured and free

How is this profound and heartfelt openness — which Paul says in Romans 8 is taken up by the Holy Spirit himself, who "intercedes for us with sighs too deep for words" — maintained in the liturgical prayers we often offer together ecumenically: prayers in which language is used as the supreme vehicle for communication with God?

We should recall that liturgical prayers in churches which have that tradition grow out of and reflect particular historical events or periods in which the deep attitudes and feelings we have been describing took the form of the words we now use in these written collective prayers. In a sense, those liturgical formulations thus oblige the Christian who uses them today to enter into a commonality of experience that embraces but goes far beyond his or her personal experience.

That struck me forcefully when I took part in a vesper service at the Armenian cathedral in Istanbul during a World Council of Churches meeting there. Some of us were invited to come forward during the liturgy to read aloud a traditional Armenian Christian prayer, translated into English for the occasion. The prayer I was assigned to read was an intercession asking God to prevent my enemies from doing me harm.

That perplexed me at first. The prayer, written by a patriarch centuries ago, clearly took for granted that the person reciting it would have enemies; and I could not imagine any personal enemy in my life to whom I could apply these lines.

So it was with some internal anguish that I made that prayer my own: "Lord, if there are people present here this evening who are confronting this kind of enmity or hostility, if there are Christians in the world facing real and powerful enemies — and I thought especially of the prisoners condemned to death for their role in the struggle for freedom in South Africa — *let my prayer be on their behalf.*"

The words of that ancient liturgical prayer forced me to set aside the relative comfort of my personal existence, to confront the reality of a world in which many people suffer daily for the sake of the kingdom of God and to raise to God a protest against that suffering and a hope that those situations would be transformed.

Thus a liturgical prayer, as the crystallization of how God's action is perceived at a given historical moment through the emotions of one worshipper, conveys the objective potential of that situation across the generations and obliges us to confront through it a wider circle of reality than we might prefer to face. Worship services which do not use that kind of liturgical prayer are too often slick, romanticized, conformed to the ethos of contemporary culture. Liturgical prayer has the power to break through that.

Having said that, I think we need also to acknowledge that these fixed prayers might become a straitjacket, preventing us from expressing the contemplation or repentance or gratitude or intercession or protest that should be evoked by a particular moment in our life or in the life of our community. Thus every liturgy ought to provide for occasions of silence and for personal prayer.

Protestants of certain traditions have difficulties with the noise of Pentecostal assemblies — everyone praying individually and simultaneously, making such a tremendous sound before God that on some occasions the neighbours have even called the police. Quite apart from the potentially salutary psychological effect of that practice of fervent prayer, it has a theological value as a recognition of the elements of community and personality before the face of God. In that togetherness all are free to bring forward their own concerns, so that what sounds to the neighbours like a mere racket might be an extraordinary manifestation of this combination of a common spirit and the awareness of particular perceptions that need to be expressed inside the community of faith.

I recall how much I was moved by this kind of praying in a worship service at an international ecumenical conference on Korean reunification in Seoul. Part of the liturgy was what is called "loud prayer". Five thousand people prayed aloud, each in his or her own words and all at the same time, expressing their hopes and anxieties about the reunification of their divided country.

To understand the significance of this unusual and intense expression of Christian spirituality, we need to remember the tragic history of Korea, split in two for more than forty years by the most impermeable frontier in the world. There is a permanent state of military alert on both sides of the 38th Parallel and families divided by that boundary — artificially imposed on them by foreign powers — cannot communicate with each other by telephone or mail, far less visit each other. Only recently have the South Korean people begun to envisage the possibility of a breakthrough, of recovering communication and encountering family, friends and fellow-Christians in the North.

Under these circumstances, a single prayer by one person on behalf of the whole congregation could scarcely have begun to express the charged emotions and utter existential involvement of all the people in the longing for and the aspiration towards reunification. The "loud prayer" accommodated an open expression of the feelings — hopeful, fearful, anxious — of all the people. Their prayers were individual, in the sense that each used his or her own words, and collective, in the sense that all were praying together along the lines set by the theme of the service, the Bible reading and hymn-singing that preceded the prayer and the encouragement of the worship leader.

It was interesting that as soon as the leader finished his own prayer it took only a minute or two for the entire congregation to come down from that peak of emotional fervour to the "orderliness" of the liturgy.

To those accustomed to completely different styles of public worship and prayer — the simplicity, say, of a Scottish Presbyterian service or the symbolically rich liturgy of the Orthodox tradition — a phenomenon like "loud prayer" might seem shocking, even chaotic. But it seemed to me more like a symphony, whose theme was defined by the concentration of the congregation's thoughts and aspirations on seeing God's hand at work and seeking insights into how God can use us to work out his purposes in history.

Especially, I think, churches that have become dry, whose prayers have become routine, might explore the possibility of allowing for such free expression by the people as a refreshment and renewal of their prayer life and their spiritual experience.

Some Pentecostal traditions also practise "praying in tongues" — a phenomenon I have witnessed though never practised. Praying in tongues is the expression — in sounds that correspond to no known language — of feelings, emotions or states of mind by people who in a moment of intense contemplation or adoration cannot find words to express what they are going through. Very often it is accompanied by an ecstatic trance.

Surely the sounds they utter have a meaning for them and for God. But they do not normally convey anything to others except an attestation of the intensity of the feelings of those going through that experience. As the Apostle Paul said, if praying in tongues is to edify the entire congregation and not just those who are praying, an interpreter is needed.

Neither in the New Testament nor in the subsequent centuries of church history has prayer in tongues been the practice of a majority. Even in those sectors of the church where it is relatively common, it is my impression that it is accepted or tolerated but less and less encouraged as something to be sought as a peculiar sign of the presence of God's Spirit.

Ecumenically, when praying in tongues happens, we should respect it, just as we respect tears, laughter, embracing and other extrovert manifestations which are meaningful to those who are going through that experience and which may, in God's mercy and wisdom, also serve to communicate with him.

Public praying

The World Council of Churches, as well as regional and national ecumenical and church bodies, occasionally calls for a special day of prayer for a specific need. An appeal may go out for intercessions on a given day on behalf of the people of Chile or of those who suffer from AIDS or for rain to end a drought. In seeking to enlist a broad spectrum of Christian people and congregations in concentrating their intercessions on a particular issue, these special days are a type of ecumenical prayer, though often the prayers are made within the context of the regular Sunday worship service of participating congregations.

In explaining the motivation and value of organizing and publicizing such special occasions of prayer, we begin by observing that when we talk about the effects of prayer we can look at the question from several different angles: What happens to the one who prays? What happens to the one for whom we are praying? What happens to those who see us praying? Finally, and most important, what is happening in God's self as a result of the prayer?

Prayer is not only the horizontal reality of coming together in a common mind, passion and expression. We have also described it as an opening of ourselves to the mystery of the reality whom we Christians call God, whom we recognize in the face of Jesus Christ. Praying is opening ourselves to the surprises of God in history.

So when we are called especially to focus our intercessions on the victims of AIDS or on people whose human rights are being trampled on by longstanding and entrenched systems of injustice, the publicity surrounding the day of prayer and the suggested liturgical forms and informational resources provided are intended to help us as worshippers to collect our minds and thoughts into a commitment of solidarity with those people.

If that happens, the concerns of the day of prayer will inevitably spill over into the days that follow. Just as I cannot pray "that all may be one" without committing myself to be more passionately involved in the search for the unity of the church, so I cannot pray "Give us this day our daily bread" without immediately sensing an obligation to open my hands in a sharing with others of the possibilities and resources at my disposal. I cannot internalize the plight of the victims of AIDS or of the people of Namibia without seeking to put my will together with the will of those in my community into a commitment to work for the alleviation of their suffering.

In chapter five we shall look in greater detail at the political significance of prayer. Suffice it to say here that this general link between praying and acting is fundamental. Prayer is a coming together around common concerns that calls the very best of us into the answer to be given to that prayer. And when a special day of prayer is called, ecumenically or nationally, it should be with the intention of informing and heightening the sense of urgency for such involvement.

Moreover, it is very important for those who are suffering in the situations that have occasioned a special prayer day to know that their fellow-Christians are supporting them with prayers. When you are in solitary confinement, and there is no way that a visitor or a telephone call or even a letter can reach you, the awareness that brothers and sisters are remembering you before God helps to liberate you from the walls of your cell, encouraging you to realize that you are not alone and that others are, at the very depth of their being and commitment, trying to be of help to you.

These two human levels are fundamental: rallying together our forces in commitment and encouraging the victims for whom we pray with the knowledge that they are being under-girded in love and solidarity.

Of course the critical question is what difference these organized and publicized prayers will make to God — and what difference God will make in our own situation as a result of them. Here of course we enter into the territory of faith. We have no handles by which to manipulate God, no magic formula to invoke him. What we have is a listening ear, as it has been given to us to understand, in Jesus Christ. By unloading our burden onto God, we receive from him the inspiration and the power to resist. By faith we also receive the conviction that all of this is working for the good of those who love God, that all of the inexplicable suffering and misery which we bring before him will become, in the mysterious way in which the Spirit of God works in history, an instrument for a new reality of justice, of peace, of *shalom*.

Consequently, by publicly promoting these special days of prayer, we are not simply engaged in a kind of political show of force to influence whatever powers might respond to our pressures. We are also registering a desperate claim, made in faith, that God will not only provide strength to endure, but that he might liberate in us and through us, and in others and through others, the imagination to change and to open doors to an overcoming of present situations of suffering and oppression.

Another form which "publicized praying" takes in some countries is the "ecumenical prayer breakfast". Government, business or labour leaders come together with pastors and laypeople from a variety of confessions for a morning meal, a meditation or address by a prominent person and prayer. While there is surely nothing wrong with Christian people coming together to pray with and for those in positions of responsibility and those whom they wish to serve, this sort of exercise is vulnerable to misuse as a platform for political proselytism or an occasion for defending political positions that are held *a priori,* without any intention of humbling laying them open to the scrutiny of prayer.

But to the extent that such prayer breakfasts seek to highlight for the community and before God our recognition that the relations between human beings and the shaping of human community are also sacred territory, they can be very important.

It seems to me, for example, that the moment of silence with which the United Nations begins its sessions is a good thing. It is surely nothing revolutionary. But it does offer delegates a chance to pause to collect their thoughts, while those who believe can bring forward in prayer the important work that faces them.

These positive comments about public praying must of course be set in dynamic relation with the injunction of Jesus: "When you pray, you must not be like the hypocrites; for they love to stand and pray in the synagogues and at the street corners, that they may be seen by men. Truly, I say to you, they have received their reward. But when you pray, go into your room and shut the door and pray to your Father who is in secret and your Father who sees in secret will reward you" (Matthew 6:5-6).

It is necessary to pray for matters of common concern to the community. It is necessary to pray with all those who are equally concerned. And that is not easy to do alone in your room. At the same time, we must maintain, even on our most public occasions of prayer, the spirit of going to our room alone — the humble spirit and lack of pretense and exhibition Jesus was commending.

The question of praying under the spotlight of the mass media is a complicated one. Sometimes the imperative of making a Christian witness and of maintaining a sense of sacredness may come into conflict. But even when we organize "prayer rallies" with prominent world figures, we need to preserve that sense of modesty.

I am reminded of the celebration of the fortieth anniversary of the World Council of Churches in the Netherlands in 1988. A solemn and beautiful worship service in the historic Old Church in the heart of Amsterdam was attended by church and ecumenical leaders from around the world and Dutch religious and political figures, including Queen Beatrix. Television cameras were not allowed inside the sanctuary to film the worship service, because the queen insisted that the spiritual practice of the sovereign is that of a human being before God, and that is something that should be protected from the limelight of public relations.

Praying with people of other faiths

We have been discussing ecumenical prayer as Christian prayer. We have emphasized that Christians pray in the name of Jesus Christ as a controlling reference, a kind of filter that purifies our limited and sinful petitions.

But prayer is a universal human phenomenon, and we should not be too quick to bracket out Christian prayer as something completely unique. Indeed, prayer is a reality for many people who profess no particular form of religious faith. It shows itself as an opening towards the unknown in moments of joy or tragedy. Somehow, we as human beings have been created for a relation with God; and that fact of our being is manifested in the most diverse religious and non-religious forms.

But if the experience of prayer or at least the impulse to pray is built into our very being, its concrete manifestation will always be conditioned by our historical, cultural, religious situation and tainted by our human sin. This conditioning and tainting with sin we also observe in the most pious Christian prayer. We cannot claim in this respect that our prayer is superior to that of people of other religious convictions or of no religious profession. Prayer calls for the total surrender of our being in the presence of God; but, as we know, such complete letting-go of ourselves is never a reality in our sinful existence.

Statistically speaking, a person who is born in India has more than three chances out of four to grow up in a Hindu environment, in both its religious and cultural manifestations. Nine times out of ten, a person born in Finland will grow up in a Lutheran environment, in both its religious and specifically Nordic cultural manifestations. Each of these persons will find a way to express the desire for communication with God that comes from being human through the thought-forms, patterns and traditions of his or her own religion and culture.

The difference between the two prayers is not at the level of manifesting spirituality in cultural forms. The person born in Finland will have a similar spectrum of possibilities for channelling his or her prayers into the cultural and religious forms of the Finnish context as the person born in India will have to do so in Indian cultural and religious forms. Nor is either of these cultural forms which conditions prayer sociologically or theologically preferable to the other.

Where we as Christians do perceive the difference, as we have said, is that Christian prayer makes a deliberate attempt to follow Jesus, to imitate his practice of prayer and to appeal to his work of redemption as that which transcends cultural limitations and purifies the sinfulness which we share with all human beings who pray.

At this point, a theologically difficult question arises. Does the God whom we know through Jesus Christ listen to the prayers of our brothers and sisters of other religious persuasions and other cultural conditionings?

In *The Book of Lights* the Jewish writer Chaim Potok puts this question powerfully. A young rabbi travelling in Japan with a companion sees an old Japanese man, prayer book in hand, slowly swaying back and forth as he stands in prayer before a Buddhist shrine. The rabbi asks his friend, "Do you think our God is listening to him?"

"I don't know," his friend replies. "I never thought of it."

"Neither did I until now," says the rabbi. "If He's not listening, why not? If He is listening, then — well, what are *we* all about?"

I believe that God in Christ was active from the beginning in creation, and it is God in Christ — who is the only God we know — who receives and listens to the aspirations of every one of his human creatures, no matter what form they use to express these.

I believe that the *Logos,* the Word, and the Spirit are active everywhere, provoking people's search for truth and aspiration towards God. Moreover, the *Logos* helps to shape the prayers of everyone and to bring those aspirations to the attention of the same Father of Jesus Christ whom we know from creation. I believe that through the same work of God which is manifested in Christ, the "screening", which we have said is consciously called forth in Christian prayer, will be provided to others.

Thus, although I cannot give a general "accreditation" to every human prayer, I would invite everyone to express himself or herself in prayerful aspiration; for in that way God has a chance to correct and to improve, because there is in the being of God a loving and welcoming disposition to receive those prayers.

Having said that, we are confronted with the ecumenically controversial question of the appropriateness of prayer and worship with people of different religious persuasions.

Even if we believe that the prayers of people of other faiths or of no religious profession aspire to be heard by the only God there is, some Christians may be unable — for cultural, sociological or religious reasons — to accept each other in a way that allows different traditions of prayer to come easily together.

Prayer demands an atmosphere of trust, of self-emptying, of total openness towards God. And when prayers are going on around us in forms that are utterly foreign and perhaps shocking to our religious sensibilities, the possibility for real concentration in our prayer may be seriously jeopardized.

Yet I also know of experiments in using, within a Christian liturgical service, prayers from the holy books of other religions. The form of their references to the divinity may be unfamiliar to Christians, but their integration into a Christian context may somehow "baptize" them into Christian spirituality.

Other experiments have used silence as a practice of prayer from different religious traditions. We respect the silence of each other, accepting that in the intimacy of our hearts and minds we come with our thought forms and patterns before the same God, but without allowing cultural or linguistic values to disrupt the prayers.

I am not talking here about syncretism — the attempt to mix together elements from many different religious traditions in order to create a new "world religion". No one would have anything to gain from that. But I think it is possible that, in living side by side with people of other religious convictions and respecting in silence their prayers, we may be drawn into the spirituality of those prayers.

In a growing number of places around the world we are now in a period of intense inter-religious living together. People of different religious persuasions are living side by side. In these diverse situations of plurality, we will unavoidably be taken into each other's spirituality.

As Christians, we need to go forward into the future in the recollection that our Lord has taught us to pray and that the apostles, imbued with the spirituality of the Jewish people, have invited us to pray in the name of Christ. Let us be trustful that this rich heritage will give us the guidance and support needed to risk an encounter with others in the hopeful expectation that our awareness will enrich their prayer life, and that their prayer life in turn will challenge us to greater faithfulness.

The churches in the ecumenical movement are profoundly divided on this issue of relations with people of other faiths. One of the most heated discussions at the WCC's Sixth Assembly in 1983 was over a document on witness, which broached the issue of interfaith relations. An early version of the paper said that, while we confess and give witness to the uniqueness of Jesus Christ, his life, death and resurrection, we also recognize God's creative hand in the religious *experience* of people of other faiths.

The debate was immediately engaged, and it was not possible to come to a consensus. The final document, as approved by a majority of the WCC Central Committee, said that "… we recognize God's creative hand in the religious *aspirations* of people of other faiths".

In a sense, this question was already put by the Apostle Paul, when he congratulated the Athenians for their altar to the unknown God. Was he congratulating them because in that "unknown God" they had, without realizing it, found the God of Jesus Christ? Or was he praising them for the perpetual openness of their search for God although they already had several gods?

The debate goes on. In 1986 Pope John Paul II invited leaders of all the world's religions to Assisi to pray for peace. There a formula was coined: "We come together to pray, but not to pray together." Every religion was invited to come to pray, but there was a separate place for the representatives of each religion.

At one level, we recognize that all our attempts to reach God are tainted with human sin. Karl Barth went so far as to say that all religions, including Christianity, are the highest manifestation of our human sinfulness, because they seek to bring God to us instead of allowing God to come to us, which coming we as Christians confess happened in the person of Jesus Christ.

I think Barth is right in saying that the very moment of our highest spiritual experiences is where we are closest to the depth of our human sinfulness. Our pride becomes part of our humility. Inevitably we try to convert our awareness of a privilege received into a badge of achievement. So when Christians pray in the name of Jesus it is with the hope that that invocation will bring the purificatory factor,to the objective reality of our prayer and the subjective reality of our very being in the act of prayer.

I do not need to sacralize the totality of the prayers of people of other religious convictions in order to accept that they are opening themselves, in the categories of their own world-view, to the same reality of God as I do. While we will need to discuss with each other our respective perceptions, conceptualizations, images of divinity, I should, in the name of my Christian conception of God — who is not a prisoner of the Christians — accept that God is receiving those expressions of prayers as the aspirations of people to reach for his mercy and his wisdom.

I cannot and may not judge how God responds to the prayer of others. What I know is that the one who has created us and planted in us some sparks of his very being is like a teacher, taking us from our different entry points into paths that are closer and closer to his loving will, which for us as Christians has been revealed in Jesus Christ.

The World Council of Churches invites observers from other religions to its major meetings. We do not ask them to lead us in prayer according to their traditions or to contribute from their spirituality to our worship and devotion. But it is obvious that Christians who are exposed daily to the spirituality of people of other religions — especially in Asia, but more and more in other parts of the world — are being permeated by those spiritualities and thereby obliged to look at their own spirituality in a new way. These Christians in turn bring to the ecumenical movement a point of contact with the spirituality of other religions that will surely have consequences for the future of the ecumenical movement.

This will continue to be a subject of ecumenical debate. We hope it will also be an occasion for growing together. More and more, I suspect, the need to "risk Christ for Christ's sake" (to take the title of a recent book by M.M. Thomas) will arise as we grow into pluralist world society, as we seek to live side by side with people of other religions and as we attempt to give our witness to the spirituality we have perceived in Jesus Christ.

Nobody is dreaming of a single world religion. But in the exchange of testimonies already taking place there will be a growing reciprocal influence of our spiritualities, which will be brought time and again to the scrutiny of what we see in the gospel of Jesus Christ.

We may add parenthetically that the question of Christians praying with Jews presents some fundamental differences from that of praying with people of other religious traditions. Because we have a shared history, there is a commonality of territory that makes it easier for Christians and Jews to pray together. Indeed, as millions of Christians and Jews read the Psalms of the Old Testament we are in a sense praying together.

Of course there are also some peculiar problems, not least of which is the history of anti-Semitism in the church. And from a theological point of view, Jews will have difficulty with our trinitarian Christian prayers. In any case, the fact that it may present fewer problems to pray with Jews does not rule out the possibility of a similar experience with people of other religions as we grow into discovering the potential commonalities that exist there.

Praying and singing

Let me conclude this overview of the varieties of ecumenical prayer by mentioning a form we sometimes overlook: singing. I would guess that most hymns written specifically for ecumenical assemblies and meetings are precisely written in the spirit of prayer and as prayers.

Some of the great hymns of the church and of the ecumenical movement take the form of affirmations of faith, confessing our unity in Christ, confessing our common faith in the Triune God. That confession comes to expression as a dialogue with God, shaded in poetic words and music. The emotions stirred up by the beauty of this expression heighten our expectation of God's presence and our awareness of the coming down of the Spirit of God to unite our voices, our minds, our wills in a common response to that presence.

Music adds another dimension to prayer in the sense that it brings with it a sense of beauty, a sense of pleasure, a sense of searching for the melody of the whole of creation. The vision of heavenly choirs in the book of Revelation seems to suggest that the ultimate expression of praise to God is in the form of singing. Music conveys prayer to the limit of our human possibilities.

As we have said, some churches retain the ancient liturgical tradition of singing the Scripture lessons and the prayers of the church. Others do not follow that tradition, perhaps aware of their limitations in terms of musical gifts, perhaps fearful that the intonation, transmitted over the generations and the centuries will become second nature, so that a certain monotony will dull the cutting edge of the Scripture, the breakthrough of the word of God.

Singing is a beautiful component in the ecumenical experience of worship. A vivid example of that was the service in Amsterdam for the fortieth anniversary of the WCC, which we mentioned above. A sung eucharistic prayer was written for the occasion. The climax of the congregational singing, accompanied by a majestic organ, was the powerful closing hymn "*A toi la gloire*", which has become an ecumenical tradition: the words expressing our common faith in the resurrected Christ in a prayer of doxology to the glory of God, set to Handel's stirring music.

It seems to me that singing is also very appropriate for those prayers in which we express our inner need for forgiveness, for cleansing, for strengthening, for sanctification. Hymns help to express the depth of our life of prayer. Although it may be somewhat more difficult to bring into our hymns the current historical challenges which confront us, there are liturgies, which deserve to be better known ecumenically, that have been written in the midst of liberation struggles or prepared for moments of great public calamity. These liturgies are able to bring into our prayer and singing the expression of our hope in God, our need of God and our claim on God for solutions to our present conflicts.

3. Learning to Pray Ecumenically

Although prayer is a matter of the inward disposition of the believer, certain passages in the New Testament suggest that praying is something we need to learn how to do. Even Jesus' disciples, whose lives were intimately and intensely associated with his on a day-to-day basis, nevertheless felt constrained to ask Jesus to teach them to pray.

It is significant that in replying to this request from his disciples, Jesus does not offer a "theology of prayer". As the story is told in Luke 11:1-4, the disciples may have been looking for a unique formula-prayer that would give them a similar badge of distinctiveness as the disciples who had been taught to pray by John the Baptist.

But instead of responding theoretically or didactically, Jesus answers the disciples' request to be taught how to pray by inviting them to pray. In the Our Father he offers them a model of what prayer should be: a contemplation of God and a concentration of our minds and wills on the vision of the kingdom, an offering of ourselves as available to be used by God.

Some biblical pointers

Because its comprehensiveness is couched in words of beautiful simplicity, the Lord's Prayer has a regular place in the liturgies of churches of many Christian confessions. This widespread familiarity also makes it suitable for use as an ecumenical prayer.

The memorable eucharistic liturgy celebrated at the Sixth Assembly of the World Council of Churches in Vancouver (1983), which drew on years of work on Baptism, Eucharist and Ministry by theologians of many traditions in the WCC Faith and Order Commission, highlights the ecumenical significance of the Lord's Prayer. It appears as the conclusion of the prayers of commemoration, just before the communion itself. The form links the reciting of the Lord's Prayer with the unity of all Christians in their "one baptism in the same Holy Spirit and the same Body of Christ", which enables them to "pray as God's sons and daughters". It is then followed by the exchange of peace, in which those who have just witnessed to their oneness by praying together give each other a sign of reconciliation and friendship.

The Lord's Prayer does not only give us words which we can make our own when we open ourselves in prayer; indeed, when we do say these words, we must be alert to the danger of this simple prayer becoming the object of the very sort of "vain repetition" to which Jesus, according to Matthew 6, presents it as an alternative. The Lord's Prayer also gives us a pattern for praying in our own words, both individually and as a group, expanding on its petitions and giving them concreteness in terms of the joys and challenges of the moment in which we are praying.

For example, during a Bible study at the WCC's 1980 World Conference on Mission and Evangelism in Melbourne, Australia, Swedish New Testament scholar Krister Stendahl offered one such "paraphrase" of the Lord's Prayer:

> O God, far above and beyond our grasp,
> yet close to us like a parent:
> Let the time come soon
> when you are recognized by all as God.
> That is, when you establish
> your supreme and good and just rule
> over your whole creation.
> Yes, let the time come soon
> when your gracious plan for salvation
> becomes a reality on earth
> as it now is in heaven.
> While we wait for that day,
> let us already now enjoy
> the foretaste of the messianic banquet
> as we share in the bread that sustains our bodies.
> In order to make us worthy of that community,
> forgive us what we have done wrong to our brothers and sisters
> as we have already forgiven those who did wrong to us;
> for we know that we are and must be
> the mutually forgiven community,
> your community of these end times.
> And see to it that we are not tested beyond our strength,
> for we know that Satan can destroy us —
> unless you rescue us out of his ferocious grip.

In considering the Lord's Prayer as a model for our personal and ecumenical praying, we can distinguish two interlinked areas. The first is the focus on God's kingdom and his justice — though even here God's concern for each of us individually is already implicit. The kingdom that is coming is the kingdom of salvation. The will that should be done is the will of love. The sanctification of God's name is the manifestation, the revealing of the children of God, for which the whole of creation, according to the Apostle Paul, is eagerly waiting (Romans 8:19).

Then comes the second part of the prayer, in which Jesus concentrates on what we might call the more human side of things: the assurance of God's presence in the everyday aspects of our dependency on him — daily bread, forgiveness of sins, liberation from temptation. But here, too, there are pointers back to the area of God's kingdom and justice. The bread for which we ask is also the sanctified bread of the communion. The forgiveness for which we plead is the entry into the kingdom of God's grace.

In other words, there is a certain interpenetration between the two parts of this prayer of Jesus. In contemplating God we are discerning the incarnation of God in Jesus Christ, who made his own the total situation of humankind. In concentrating our attention on the concrete needs of humankind, we are seeing through to the Father's concern and care for all his creatures.

We need to learn to pray. And we learn to pray by praying, by discerning, in the model provided by Jesus, the way to go forward in opening ourselves to the contemplation of God in Christ and to the bringing into that contemplation of the needs in our life and in the life of all humanity.

As important as this "practising of prayer" is, however, we should not forget that other passages of Scripture say that the Holy Spirit is the one who brings forth prayer in the believer. This is a humbling but reassuring reality when we are inclined to suspect that the range of human needs we should bring before the Lord vastly exceeds our ability to articulate them in prayer. In fact, when we enter into the communion with God which is prayer, we are entering into the internal dialogue of the Trinity. The Holy Spirit orders and perfects our incomplete and incoherent expressions of anguish and hope and makes them present in the very being of God.

So we are called not only to learn how to pray but to invoke the help of the Spirit in our prayer. As we pray for the Spirit to teach us to pray, we are taken into the reality of a relationship with God which we cannot explain or articulate in a neat formula, but which is nevertheless an existential reality in which we invite others to participate as well.

This is a paradox that comes out of our awareness of the otherness of God, our Christian consciousness of a God who in Christ has taken the initiative. We invite people to come to pray and at the same time we say that it is God who calls forth from us the response of prayer to his love, grace, presence which was already there in our life.

Perhaps we can begin to understand this by analogy with human love and friendship. The love which unites me to my mother is of course a disposition in myself. But it is a disposition that emerges naturally out of my awareness and experience of my mother's love, which has preceded my response to her. Something similar happens in all my relations of love or friendship. It is not just that I love my wife; it is that her presence helps to generate the reality of that love.

Of course, such human examples are imperfect as an explanation of our relation with God, who is a reality beyond our capacity to describe. But what God has wanted to give us in Jesus Christ, according to the message of the Bible, is a conviction that when we open ourselves and try to look into the direction of God, something happens from the other side that helps us to pray as we did not think possible for us to do.

When we pray ecumenically, it is inevitable that this attempt to open ourselves to God takes place in public, often in a crowd. But that brings us back to the question we touched on in the previous chapter. In the Sermon on the Mount — the context in which Matthew sets the Lord's Prayer — Jesus advises his followers to pray in their rooms, with the door shut. Is there a contradiction here between our ecumenical practice and the words of Jesus?

Jesus and his disciples, as pious Jews, shared in the life and discipline of public prayer in the synagogue. But Jesus recognized the potential of misuse and abuse in public prayer, which can conceal spurious motives or attitudes of superiority. What he criticizes is showing off, the religiosity of the intense prayers which some of his contemporaries were making on the streets in order to be seen by others. Using the concrete and picturesque language by which he often conveyed spiritual insights, Jesus makes a contrast between these florid prayers out in the open and the simple, quiet, unnoticed praying which, he says, God will hear and answer.

What Jesus has in mind may be the cellar, the place where the family's daily food was preserved. Thus he is suggesting that when we pray we should hide from visibility and the temptations that it brings. Aware of the temptation that surrounds our prayer life, Jesus was trying to protect his disciples from it. The antidote to visible religiosity, which imposes itself on those around, is an attitude of humility, hiding oneself for a quiet struggle with God without succumbing to the pressures of the surrounding society.

But we should not interpret Jesus' life and teachings on prayer only through this text, which accents an aspect closely tied up with his own social and cultural context. We need also to think of our own situation.

I sometimes suspect that if Jesus were teaching today in the cities of Western Europe, he would invite praying Christians to come out of their cellars to stand in front of the banks and businesses and embassies and government buildings on the square, to have the courage to make public their recognition of God's presence and their faith in the reality of communion with God which prayer makes possible.

The temptation for Jesus' contemporaries was showing off their religiosity. Our temptation, especially in industrialized urban societies, is more likely to be middle-class self-restraint, hiding our religious convictions and practices. And this erodes the potential for testimony which is inherent in public prayer.

I do not want to make too much of small things like praying before a meal in a restaurant. But I think that this small gesture in itself points to the wider implications of public manifestations of faith, for example, at critical moments in the life of a people when their anguish must somehow be brought to the attention of God, thus also drawing the attention of public opinion to the critical issues at stake.

Now how do we hold together that emphasis of Jesus on the privacy of our prayer with the fact that the ecumenical movement prays visibly and publicly, sometimes even with television cameras recording every petition? Beyond the question of historical context which we mentioned above, we should recognize that religion in the life of Jesus was fundamentally a community affair. He came from the Jewish tradition, where the whole people of God was called to repentance, to faith, to worship in the temple or in the synagogue. He confirmed his belonging to that tradition by regularly attending services in the synagogue and by creating a community of prayerful support with his own disciples.

So Jesus does not reject collective prayer. What he wants is to protect that prayer from the temptation to self-destructive hypocrisy of a practice which by its focus on exhibiting piety loses the possibility of being prayer, because it is no longer centred on God, as Christian prayer must be.

Through the centuries the gathering of Christians on the first day of the week has been a celebration of the risen Lord and a prayer for his visible coming in the words, "Maranatha, come Lord Jesus". There is no contradiction between individual prayer closed in a given place and coming together to pray. Ecumenically, this coming together to pray preserves the best of Jewish-Christian tradition and at the same time seeks to be an honest opening of the life of the community, across all the different boundaries that would divide us, to correction and inspiration from God.

Earlier we noted that some people may wonder whether we do not spend too much time in prayer in our ecumenical encounters. And in the passage from Matthew we have been discussing, Jesus gives short shrift to the idea — which he attributes to "the Gentiles" — that our prayers "will be heard for their many words". Yet the apostle, in a series of injunctions to a first-century congregation, calls on them to "pray constantly" (1 Thessalonians 5:17). What might it mean, ecumenically, for us to "pray without ceasing"?

I can imagine two different but complementary meanings for this familiar text. One is a sort of figurative understanding, which would see the whole of life as prayer. Our ongoing ecumenical expression of love towards our neighbour by solidarity with the marginal is a service to God and is thus a dimension of our religious conviction. Whatever Christians undertake together ecumenically — to proclaim the good news of salvation, to bind up the wounds of people, to struggle against racism and injustice, to renew the church — should all be understood in these terms, so that all of ecumenical life is a life of prayer.

Without disregarding the element of truth in that interpretation, we should go on to observe that we are subject — ecumenically as well as individually — to the ambiguities of history and the limits of our own intellect and psychology. We need moments in which we stop to ask ourselves, "What do we really believe? What is the sense of our actions? What is the direction we want to go?" At those moments of reflection, we are in a dialogue with God that is really prayer.

A second possible interpretation is the monastic one, perhaps through developing disciplines of prayer so that one can do work (especially manual labour) almost automatically while one's mind continues in prayer, remembering holy things and the symbols of faith, or, more traditionally, through the monastic vocation, concentrated in certain individuals but at the service of the whole community.

I think there is room for a new ecumenical appraisal of monasticism as a particular contribution, offered by a sector of the church, of permanent intercessory prayer for the rest of the community. "Prayer without ceasing", prayer vigils (such as the one undertaken around the clock during the WCC's Sixth Assembly, praying for every Assembly participant by name) are undertaken in steady support of others.

At the same time, let us be sure that in our daily life we assume the responsibilities that belong to building up human society. A pilot may pray, but while responsible for a planeload of passengers, what he or she must be doing "without ceasing" is keeping a watchful eye on all the controls and gauges in the cockpit. This form of faithful service is what is demanded during the flight; and prayer before or afterwards will be a request for the ability to preserve that faithfulness.

I think the central intention of the apostle's injunction is: be sure that you understand whatever you are and whatever you do in the horizons of the kingdom of God, that is, in its intrinisic relation to God's will or purpose. Finally, there are no secular events.

So to pray without ceasing is to assume at every moment and in every circumstance that there is a hidden relation between this and God's purpose. Even as we are drinking coffee with a few friends, can we somehow understand this fellowship, which may be very superficial, as a sign, a symbol, a foretaste, of that fuller communion that we call the kingdom of God?

Personal and collective prayer

Some of the Psalms in the Old Testament are quite clearly outpourings of solitary prayer. Others are equally obviously intended for use on very public occasions: the coronation of a king, the festive celebration of gratitude at the time of the harvest, the expectant songs which pilgrims sang as they made their way to the temple in Jerusalem. To read the Psalms is to be struck time and again by the strange and beautiful juxtaposition of individual prayers with prayers representing the whole people.

Clearly, the tendency when we come to pray together in our congregations or in ecumenical encounters is to focus on the social and collective dimensions of our Christian lives and obedience. We take up into our prayers the problems and challenges we have identified together. We denounce the sins that are affecting people in our local or global community. We pray for corporate forgiveness of our corporate neglect, lack of courage, even profitable complicity in the structures of injustice and oppression.

Ecumenically, therefore, we may tend to overlook the individual cry for forgiveness, the denunciation of individual sins and the call for personal repentance. Indeed, critics of the World Council of Churches sometimes speak out sharply against what they see as our overemphasis on denouncing and confronting social evils at the expense of attending to individual ethical issues and personal spiritual commitment.

Besides the observation that this distinction between the "personal" and the "social" is notoriously difficult to draw with any precision, one can make a number of points in response to this criticism. The WCC is a council of churches, which means that those who participate in its activities are doing so first and foremost not as individual Christians, but as representatives of their churches and Christian communities or as persons with a special expertise that can help to illuminate an issue on the churches' agenda. Even if some of these issues may have an obvious individual dimension — alcoholism and drug abuse, for example — any ecumenical activity or encounter will have a "collective" focus on how this issue is a shared concern across the churches and Christian communities represented.

Moreover, as an ecumenical organization the WCC does not seek — and does not have the competence — to fulfill all the functions and ministries of a church. Its members are churches, not individuals. The WCC encourages and tries to support churches in undertaking their evangelistic task, but it does not itself send out missionaries to proclaim the gospel and call people to conversion. It speaks out with deep concern against a wide variety of sins, but it does not itself undertake a ministry of personal pastoral care to individuals who are sinning — not because it does not care about these individuals but because it is not the primary vocation of a council of churches to minister to them.

We may perhaps also cite psychological explanations for the tendency of our ecumenical prayer life to focus on collective problems and concerns. With all the vast and seemingly intractable problems facing large groups of people in every part of our world today, we may be inclined to suppose that when we come together ecumenically it is tasteless or embarrassing or unworthy to make too much of our individual problems and joys.

When millions will go to bed tonight hungry, do I dare to complain publicly about my backache? In a world where people are denied basic human rights only because of the colour of their skin, should I not restrict expressions of my anxiety over tensions in my own family to private devotions? With people in so many countries suffering under the burden of battered economies, what right do I have to pray in the presence of others for less drudgery in my well-paid and secure job?

Then, too, the diversity which makes participation in the ecumenical forum so rich an experience does not by itself bridge the daunting gaps of culture and language it comprises. Even with the best of intentions, we may be discouraged from allowing the depth of our personal commitments and doubts to be brought forward ecumenically. In any case, the ability and willingness to testify and pray in public about matters of profound personal importance varies widely among the most devout and faithful Christians, according to how introverted or extroverted their personalities are.

But however valid these explanations for the fact that ecumenical prayer and devotion accent issues of collective concern and pay relatively scant attention to matters of individual concern, we cannot escape the fact that both the personal and the social belong together in the discipline of Christian prayer, and we need to be sure that they remain together in the discipline of ecumenical prayer.

I recall from growing up in the Latin American Methodist tradition that we used to have spiritual retreats in youth camps, in which collective devotions were followed by ten or twenty minutes of individual, personal reading of the Bible and prayer. I always found that a useful combination; and something of that must be preserved in the ecumenical movement.

One thing I have found helpful in recent Assemblies of the World Council of Churches is that the thousands of participants are divided into small groups of 12 to 15 people. At regular intervals during the Assembly, they come together to read the Bible, to pray and to share their concerns in this more intimate and personal setting.

Similarly, in the Ecumenical Centre in Geneva, we have a collective worship service for the entire staff and visitors each Monday morning. But every day a smaller group of people comes together for a few minutes of intercession, a time of more personal and intimate prayer bringing before God individual needs and hopes and expectations.

Something of that rhythm needs to be preserved. In the liturgical richness of the ecumenical movement we should find expression for both the individual within the community and the community as that which embraces all the individuals in it. But the tension will always be there, and we need to be aware of it.

Spiritual disciplines

Several times in this brief chapter the fact that prayer is a matter of spiritual discipline has come to the fore. Over the centuries, a rich Christian literature has grown up on this deepest aspect of our human existence. If the preponderance of these guides for spirituality have focused on the individual in his or her relationship with God, it remains true, as we have said, that we must hold our individual spirituality together with corporate expressions of spirituality, whether within the limited and immediate context of a prayer group or the vast and sometimes abstract scope of the *oikoumene,* the whole people of God.

Let me conclude this chapter with some comments on two forms of ecumenical spiritual discipline which are — or can be — intimately related to the prayer which we have described as a central ecumenical reality.

One is Bible reading. It is sometimes suggested that reading the Bible is in fact more important than praying. After all, in the Bible God is speaking to us, whereas in prayer we are "merely" speaking to God. I find such a distinction between praying and reading the Bible misleading.

In fact, of course, one can read the Bible in many different ways, not necessarily as the Word of God. One can read it as a more or less historical record from which to draw insights into the life of ancient cultures and civilizations. One can read it as a masterpiece of world literature. One can read it as a collection of edifying or even entertaining stories. Each of these ways of reading the Bible has its distinct values, but in none of them is the Bible yet the Word of God "speaking to us".

The Bible becomes the Word of God when the presence of God suddenly breaks through it — and at that moment the person who is reading the Bible is in fact praying. A conscious act of petitionary prayer may not be a prerequisite for reading the Bible as the Word of God, but no reading of the Bible that is an encounter with the Word of God happens apart from the situation of prayer. It is a recognition of this which lies behind the practice in many Christian liturgical traditions of preceding the Scripture reading and sermon with an explicit "prayer of illumination".

Reading the Bible is fundamental within the Christian community precisely to build up the criteria, the screening, the controlling factors for our spirituality, to prevent our human reality, shaped by our culture and tradition and tainted by sin, from taking the lead role in our life of prayer. In the ecumenical community this need to read the Bible together time and again is perhaps even more acute, so as to break through the walls of our separate confessions and cultures, so as to denounce our sins, so as to allow the Spirit of God to be fully present and understood in our consciousness.

The Bible is a school of prayer. On almost every page, there is manifestation of prayer. Of course, our attention is immediately drawn in this connection to the Psalms, the book of prayer *par excellence*. But all of the prophetic books record a permanent dialogue with God, often in the form of protest. This struggle, this fight with God, we have said earlier, is very important for us to recover as a dimension of our prayer.

Besides being the cradle of our prayer, its guiding and controlling factor, its inspiration, the Bible is, especially for the collective prayer we do ecumenically, a collection of shared images, a sourcebook of our common Christian memory, which can help to unify the prayers we articulate together as a worldwide community of Christians.

A second spiritual discipline that many Christians have found important for their prayer life is fasting.

Let me begin by saying that this is not a practice I have inherited from my Latin American Methodist background. Historically, Protestant churches have generally not been very keen on fasting — I suppose out of reaction against what they have seen as the mistaken and theologically dangerous idea that self-inflicted punishment now will earn merit before God later. But in the past few years I have rediscovered fasting in the practice of the ecumenical family, especially in the practice of the Orthodox Church.

I have found some helpful insights in the "ecclesiastical principles concerning fasting" which were drafted by representatives of fourteen Eastern Orthodox churches in 1986 as part of the long-term preparatory process for a great synod of these churches.

Noting that the New Testament portrays fasting "as a means of abstinence, repentance and spiritual uplift", this document says it is "indissolubly linked with unceasing prayer and sincere repentance... Fasting without good deeds is nothing, particularly in our era, when the unequal and unjust distribution of property deprives whole peoples even of their daily bread."

But fasting is not just a matter of giving up certain foods. St Basil said that "true fasting consists of driving out evil, controlling one's tongue, abstaining from anger, giving up desires, slander, lying, perjury"; and Clement of Alexandria noted that "food has never made us either more or less righteous. Fasting has a deeper meaning. Just as food is the symbol of life and the absence of food the symbol of death, so we ought to fast in order to die to this world and after that, having received divine nourishment, live in God."

The document also cites St Gregory Palamas, who saw a Christ-centred significance in the spiritual character of fasting: "If you fast, not only will you undergo Christ's passion and die with him, but you will also arise again and reign with him for eternity; for if, by means of this fast, you have become a being similar to him through a death resembling his, you will participate in the resurrection and inherit life in him."

Understood in this way fasting can be seen as a symbolic way to participate in the situation of suffering people, to promote a total empathy between their situations and ours. By imposing physical and psychological limitations on us, fasting helps us to reflect more deeply on the issues they are praying about. Fasting as a spiritual exercise from the biblical tradition is being recovered as a methodology to help us psychologically to come closer to those who are suffering and thus to raise a prayer and commitment that will be more passionate, more substantial.

I still need to explore fasting as a personal spiritual discipline for my own meditation. Would it not be good for my own spiritual life, for the reappraisal of my own identity, to go through periods from time to time when the emptiness of my physical existence could be an instrument to help my self-reflection?

As a Protestant, of course, this seems to me to be risky theological territory. I do not want to limit God's power to these limits of my own personal psychological preparation for prayer. God cannot be dependent on how I prepare myself to be receptive to him.

At the same time, for the encounter with God's Spirit, I want to offer whatever disposition could be in me. Since fasting has been a discipline of the church over the centuries, why not give it a chance? Not by making it law, but by recognizing it as an instrument in the arsenal of human disciplines that might be helpful for growing into the image of Jesus Christ.

O Lord Jesus, stretch forth thy wounded hands
in blessing over thy people,
to heal and to restore, and to draw them to thyself
and to one another in love.

(Middle East)

O God, thou art one; make us one

O God, forgive us
for bringing this stumbling block of disunity
to a people who want to belong to one family.
The church for which our Saviour died is broken,
and people can scarcely believe
that we hold one faith and follow one Lord.
O Lord, bring about the unity
which thou hast promised,
not tomorrow or the next day, but today.

(Africa)

O God, thou art one; make us one

O Lord, forgive the sins of thy servants.
May we banish from our minds all disunion and strife.
May our souls be cleansed
of all hatred and malice towards others.
And may we receive the fellowship of the Holy Meal
in oneness of mind and peace with one another.

(India)

O God, thou art one; make us one

Just as the bread which we break
was scattered over the earth,
was gathered in and became one,
bring us together from everywhere
into the kingdom of your peace.

(Epistle to Diognetus)

O God, thou art one; make us one

"Make us one: prayers for unity from many countries", from the
Worship Book for the WCC's Sixth Assembly, Vancouver, 1983

4. Problems with Prayer

For many of our contemporaries the Christian practice of prayer seems old-fashioned and quaint, a throwback to a bygone age, perhaps even a bit neurotic and out-of-touch with reality.

As we mentioned earlier, even among people who share many of the concerns of the ecumenical movement, some would question the relatively large attention devoted to prayer, worship, Bible study and other spiritual exercises at ecumenical meetings and conferences. Isn't this a distraction from more urgent elements of our common calling? Would it not be better to spend more time in wrestling with, speaking out and strategizing for action in the face of the suffering caused by injustice and conflict, by hunger and disease, by damage to the environment which jeopardizes our very future on this planet?

It is clear that the kind of prayer we have been talking about, a complete openness before God, faces many obstacles. Some of these obstacles come from within ourselves, for the act of prayer does not exempt us from either the limitations of our human finiteness or our sinfulness. Other obstacles come from the world around us. Again and again, we are reminded that the area of the unexplained, for which one might wish to invoke supernatural explanations and divine interventions, continues to shrink in the face of the growth of human understanding in natural and social sciences.

And so we may hear the apostle's exhortation to "pray without ceasing", but our actual experience when we try to pray is that described by a couplet of Shakespeare in *Hamlet:* "My words fly up, my thoughts remain below:/ Words without thoughts never to heaven go." Or our acts of devotion are misunderstood — as was the experience of Hannah in the Old Testament, who prayed so fervently for a son that Eli the priest thought she was drunk.

We need to take seriously both internal and external obstacles to prayer. Neither as individual Christians nor as an ecumenical movement may we flaunt our practice of prayer as a badge of achievement, a token of our spiritual status for which we need give no account to those who question it or find themselves unable to share in it.

Prayer and fantasy

Even everyday idioms speak of prayer in a way that suggests it belongs more to the world of fantasy than to reality. Discussing a football team's chances to win the league championship, we may say glibly, "They have nothing left but a prayer" (or, worse, "They don't have a prayer"). One hears talk of "praying for a miracle". Indeed, the 19th-century Russian writer Ivan Turgenev goes so far as to say somewhere that "whatever a man prays for, he prays for a miracle. Every prayer reduces itself to this 'Great God, grant that twice two not be four.'"

I recall vividly a special prayer service we held at the Ecumenical Centre in 1988 which was very much undertaken with the sense that we had "nothing left but a prayer". It was the afternoon before the scheduled execution of six black people in South Africa — "the Sharpeville Six", as they had come to be known — who had been convicted of murder following the killing of the mayor of Sharpeville several years earlier. Under South African law, they were liable to conviction for murder because they had been part of a crowd whose intentions had been murderous and whose actions had resulted in a killing, even though the government did not prove that any of the six had personally caused the death of the mayor.

Everything seemed to indicate that the execution would be carried out the next morning. Every possible appeal, through governments, international organizations and national bodies in South Africa had been tried without success. What remained?

Under the circumstances, our despair as Christians in the ecumenical family was the same despair felt by people without any particular religious convictions who shared our abhorrence of apartheid and this particular case of its injustice. There was nothing they could do, nothing we could do. The only thing that remained was prayer; and so we prayed. Were we expecting a miracle? Yes. Did we rationally suppose that a miracle would happen? No. So prayer was the last resort. We had nothing left but a prayer.

But beyond our petition for the immediately important thing, the saving of the lives of those six people, we were able in our prayer to frame our anguish and despair, our protest and rage, in the context of a hidden source of meaning, a revealed source of hope. We opened up a new instance of hope.

Naturally, we could speak, in terms of the classical Christian doctrine of the resurrection of the dead, of our firm confidence that those lives about to be snuffed out by the powers of this world would not be finally lost, because we believe in God's care for them even beyond death, opening the potential and promise of eternal life.

We could also look to the more immediate future in this world, bringing into our prayer the expectation that this terrible execution would, in the context of South Africa, sound a particularly forceful cry into the ears of the powerful and a particularly compelling invitation rallying the forces of the weak and oppressed, so that like the Christian martyrs of old, the blood of these six people could, in tragic and mysterious ways, become a seed from which new possibilities of justice and reconciliation could grow.

When we pray in situations which are humanly speaking so apparently hopeless, we do so with the petition of Jesus from the Garden of Gethsemane in our hearts and on our lips: "Nevertheless, not as I will, but as thou wilt" (Matthew 26:38).

But in praying for the will of God to be done, as in the case of the Sharpeville Six, we are in no way suggesting that we believe that it is God's will for innocent people to be killed. In the ministry of Jesus Christ we see clearly that the will of God is never the acceptance of demon-possession or of the oppression of the common people. It is a liberating will which pronounces a word of healing and issues a call to responsibility. The will of God for which we are asking is the will of his kingdom of justice. The will of God to which we appeal is the multiplication of the power of those who are powerless into the shaping of another future.

"Your will be done", as Krister Stendahl observes, is a prayer, not a disguised moral admonition to accept things as they come, no matter what. It is not an expression of fatalism. "Your will be done" means "Let us use, let us hope that God will use even this tragic rebuke to his love and lordship as an instrument for the opening of the way toward the kingdom that is coming".

So "your will be done" is similar to the question Paul raised on the road to Damascus. When the heavenly vision confronted him, he could only fall on his knees and say, "O Lord, what do you want me to do?" To pray for God's will to be done is to ask God to teach us *how* that will can be done, *how* the present situation can be transformed into a new beginning in the direction of the kingdom of God and his justice, which is the final manifestation of God's will.

Some people would argue that adding "your will be done" to our prayers rules out any discussion of whether or not the prayer is answered, because whatever happens is God's will.

At one level that is correct. Traditional Christian piety has always held that every prayer is answered, though the answer is not always in accord with the wishes or wisdom of the person praying. That is a very clear and rational position. Perhaps, though, it is *too* clear and rational. I think we need to keep open the question of answer to prayer precisely because prayer is not magic. We do not have a handle with which to control God. Human freedom within history has created a sinful reality which will not be finally eliminated before the consummation of the age. In our prayers we ask God to reveal himself within this penultimate situation; and that may take the form of a penultimate solution.

More spiritually dangerous is praying "your will be done" because we do not really care very much about what we are praying for. Then we are praying as if we were ordering something we don't really need from a department store: if it arrives, fine; if it doesn't, no problem.

I suspect that too many of our prayers for suffering people are of this detached variety. Rather than struggling with God about their pain, we pray routinely and mechanically with formulas that are all-too-familiar: "be with the people who are sick", "comfort the sorrowing", "sustain the suffering", "feed those who are hungry"... and "your will be done".

Maybe we do not struggle with God in prayers like these because we are not really struggling with ourselves. Consider, for example, the situation in South Africa we have been discussing. How can we as rich Christians in wealthy countries be so concerned with imminence of the execution of these brothers and sisters while remaining indifferent to the suffering caused because our country wants to maintain lucrative banking and commercial relations with South Africa?

So our ecumenical prayer for the six South Africans who were scheduled to die — when it seemed that there was nothing left but a prayer — was no simple petition: "Lord, save them somehow if it is your will." Indeed, this passionate plea was built into the prayer, along with expectation and hope that God would respond with actions of liberation that we could see and celebrate. But at the same time we were acknowledging our complicity with the powers that were preparing to lead those six young people to their death. Far from not caring, we were caring in respect of the mystery of God who has granted the gift of freedom and with that gift the condition for all the evil in the world.

Love for those six people, whose fate was somehow becoming our fate, awareness of our own guilt and acknowledgement of our powerlessness were combined with a dream, an assurance, a faith that God could work in this situation, whether through the liberation or the death of those six people, in such a way that South African history would not be closed by this event. We were reminded of the stirring words of Allan Boesak at the WCC's Sixth Assembly: you cannot emigrate from history; you cannot escape from the judgement of God. Our prayer was also a cry for the manifestation of that judgment in history.

As a matter of fact, as we were gathering in the chapel for this special prayer service came the first unconfirmed word from South Africa that a judge, because of doubts about the reliability of one of the prosecution witnesses, had ordered an eleventh-hour stay of execution.

That of course did not "prove" the effectiveness of the prayers which had been made earlier for the Sharpeville Six to be spared. At the same time, precisely because we do not see prayer as a magic technique to manipulate God, word of the stay of execution did not eliminate the need for our prayer service or even essentially change the character of the prayers we offered.

So when we say in a given historical situation that prayer is the only thing that remains, it is not necessarily the case that we are simply indulging ourselves in a fantasy.

But fantasy is an ever-present danger to our prayer life. We are prone to manipulate prayer for our own satisfaction. We are tempted to be like the Pharisee in Jesus' parable. Rejoicing that we have everything we need in life, whether physical or spiritual, we pray only in order to bask in self-congratulation.

That kind of fantasy is tragic. But I do not consider it a fantasy when the eyes of faith look beyond an historical cul-de-sac in search of resources which, rationally speaking, are not at our disposal.

The difference between the person of faith and the non-believer is not a question of intelligence. The difference is that the person of faith opens up another instance which might, at the level of pure rationality, be described as a fantasy, but which gives strength and consolation, keeps us in the struggle and in the end is not fantasy at all, for it may be that our cries of despair are like Jesus' cry on the cross: "My God, my God, why have you forsaken me?" — which receives its ultimate answer in the mystery and power of the resurrection.

Prayer and secularism

Such an understanding of prayer will, of course, not readily resonate in a secular scientific, technological society (though one is inclined to add that in many parts of the world — East and West, South and North — society is not in fact as secular as is usually claimed).

If I try to explain this opening of my being to dimensions of reality which escape rational perception in terms that satisfy "secular" people, I may be obliged to give an account of prayer that will not satisfy my own Christian understanding of prayer. At the same time, such an effort to spell out to a non-Christian friend in secular terms what I mean by prayer is valid only if it opens the way to a testimony to Jesus Christ. In the final analysis, what may produce curiosity about prayer in my secular friend can only be the concentration of his or her attention on the person of Jesus Christ — not my philosophical or theological explanation of the reality of prayer.

Nevertheless, it is perhaps worthwhile, particularly in the context of the ecumenical movement, which is deeply engaged in the struggles of everyday life in every part of the world and at the same time is not reluctant to be seen at prayer, to venture a kind of "secular" explanation of prayer.

The problem of prayer is basically the problem of the reality of God. For genuinely secular minds, God is for all practical purposes a remnant of old perceptions of life, for which there is no place in a so-called scientific understanding of reality.

If our worldview allows for a dimension of reality not accessible to rational means of understanding and discourse, if we admit the reality of a frame of reference that gives meaning to the whole, a dimension of experience that opens up windows of understanding beyond the passing events of every day, if we admit the reality of freedom in an organized and orderly universe, we open the door for a relation among free beings and assume the potential rationality of what we call prayer as related to the dimension of freedom that we detect in the whole of reality.

To my secular friend, I will explain that prayer is a way to open myself to dimensions of existence which have been manifested in history in the life of Jesus Christ, and within which I see a summary of all the good, the beauty, the values that everyone recognizes as constituting our humanness.

I will also speak of the dimension of freedom in human existence, of the impossibility of a universe that is closed in on itself. This dimension of freedom in us, the capacity to create, the capacity to be a poet, the capacity to aspire to human relations at the level of love, which escapes all scientific measuring and laboratory analysis — this entire realm is the presupposition of my prayer, which is an attempt to attune my freedom to the source of being in the freedom of the whole universe, that is the freedom of God, the Creator of this universe.

So I will invite my friend to consider that the whole of reality is far richer than that part of it which we can control; that the totality of being is more vast than what we can express within our secular categories; that in the person of Jesus Christ there is a dimension of being which provokes my wonder, which in turn becomes prayer; that the search for meaning, the search for help, the search for someone to participate in my joy is the existential dimension that calls forth a response in prayer.

At this point, the conversation with my secular friend should become very personal. We should come to a moment of confronting together the reality of a joy that seeks its echo in the totality of reality, or the dimension of pain and suffering, symbolized by death, which demands that my questions be subsumed under the ultimate question of the meaning of reality.

Up to a certain point, in other words, I can adjust my categories and my vocabulary to those of my secular friend. But finally I am obliged to break through the barrier and to pray for, and if possible with, my secular friend.

Those who question the relevance of prayer in a secular world often do so in terms of a "God of the gaps". God, according to this explanation, is a hypothesis that believers bring in to explain anything they cannot account for scientifically. But as science deepens its understanding of the universe, this area of what cannot be explained becomes ever smaller, meaning that there is less and less need to invoke the presumed existence and activity of God.

For example, whereas people of an earlier generation or century might have prayed for deliverance from illness or the ravages of an epidemic, our current understanding of biology and its practical applications in preventive or curative medicine, holistic techniques, better nutrition or sanitation suggests that we must focus our ministry of healing in these areas.

In fact, such a claim probably overstates our knowledge of the resources for healing that operate in the universe — as is evident from the renascence in the past few years of interest in traditional healing through herbal medicines. Nevertheless, it is true that, from the point of view of our present knowledge of science, one could interpret some of the miracles the gospels record Jesus as performing as indications of something not at all extraordinary.

What is extraordinary is that two thousand years ago Jesus could have used methodologies that are ordinary today — techniques which involve an understanding of the psychosomatic, for example. I can leave open the possibility that a growth in our knowledge might fully explain tomorrow what I call a miracle today. From my perspective as a Christian that eliminates neither my thankfulness to God for a miracle today nor my belief in a God who works through the organization of nature, which is also the fruit of his hands.

The difficult problem is why not everyone is healed. Why does one person give testimony of healing while another, in the same circumstances, remained ill? Why was my life spared on the battlefield while my friend fell at my side, even though he had more faith (if faith can be quantified) than I?

Let me be more specific. I protest against the propaganda of preachers of healing who advertise that healings are taking place here, in this particular place. If a healing does take place, the only thing to do is to render heartfelt thanks to God. But that manifestation of his Spirit in healing is *free*. It is not something any human being can control for himself or herself. We cannot command healing. We are invited to pray for the healing of our neighbours. And in the life of any Christian, there are moments in which a particular manifestation of God's healing power, for which we do not have a rational explanation, has been real.

God is Spirit, and the Spirit is freedom. God operates through a combination of factors of change. In general, there are three of these factors. One is mechanical linkage: if the right two elements are put together, it will always produce fire. Another is chance: sometimes when the two elements come together to produce fire, they are exposed to a third element and a new reality comes to life. The third is purpose. Even animal behaviour indicates a purpose that is able to affect the habitat to a certain degree; and, as far as human beings are concerned, of course, this factor of purpose is fundamental.

Here and there God, who works through all three of these dimensions of reality, may produce a signpost that escapes our capacity to explain and understand. We are thankful when the manifestation is a positive one like healing, but we cannot pretend to control God or to oblige God always to produce such a result — for total chaos would follow if purpose were the only factor in reality.

This is a subject about which we cannot afford to be too dogmatic. In recent years, physicists and cosmologists have been engrossed in studying the nature of matter at sub-atomic levels, developing and testing theories of particles and forces undreamed of a generation ago. A few theologians have sought to pursue the implications of these fascinating new theories for our understanding of the origins and workings of the universe. Thus new horizons of insight may be opened up into the mystery and potential for change that is the object of so many of the petitions in our prayers. In this area, in which we can still speak only hesitantly and tentatively, there is a challenge for the ecumenical community to wrestle together for understanding, so that we may continue to "give an account of the hope that is in us" in terms that speak to the needs and aspirations of the people of the 20th — and the 21st — century.

It is possible, then, that an apparent healing in response to prayer may later be explained as triggered by interacting factors of which we were not aware at the time. More difficult to explain than healings in response to prayer — and more common ecumenically — is prayer for social and historical changes, which must happen through the will and action of other people.

If we pray publicly for the release of people condemned to death in South Africa, we are appealing to God to intervene. At the same time, we ourselves are intervening by creating a certain public opinion. We affirm by faith that some events produced in history are responsive to our prayer — without being able to credit that in any objective way.

Long after the Hebrew people left Egypt and crossed the Red Sea and passed through the wilderness on the way to the Promised Land, sages and poets and prophets reflected on that story. They discerned clearly in these events God's power and wisdom leading his people. But the contemporary sociologist or historian who looks at the same phenomena sees them as the movements of a nomadic people searching for better water and land.

The social scientist analyzes historical evidence with the tools of his or her respective science. Fair enough. But the eyes of faith discern there a dimension of reality which is expressed in the form of a testimony. The only way other people can understand this latter explanation is by coming to the experience of faith which is produced by the contemplation of Jesus Christ.

Prayer and alienation

We have been looking at prayer from the inside, as it were, seeking as those open to the transcendent will of God to give an account of our practice of prayer which turns aside the argument that it is merely wishful thinking, an exercise in manipulating ourselves or others to accept as true that which we would like to believe.

But we must recognize also that there are people who would like to pray but cannot. With the world as it is, with their own lives the way they are, some people are simply unable to open themselves to the dimension of transcendence. Again, Shakespeare, in *Macbeth,* puts the experience of many people in a few vivid words: "I had most need of blessing, and 'Amen' stuck in my throat."

What is called for here is more an expression of solidarity than the solution to an intellectual problem. We can make no response whatsoever to this kind of alienation apart from an attitude of respectful willingness first to hear the person out. Often, his or her problem with prayer stems from a very painful personal experience; and pious testimonies about our own relationship with the Lord will be of no help to him or her at all.

In the wilderness of life there are moments of tremendous dryness which must be lived through. We are called to accompany our fellow human beings who are having such an experience, never giving up hope that at some point light and warmth from God will come to manifest themselves, enabling them to overcome those tragic experiences or to see them in another light.

Of course our encounter with persons going through this kind of difficulty or alienation will elicit our prayers *for* them. In some circumstances, it may also be appropriate to pray *with* them, not in an attitude of superiority, which would be calamitous, but in the belief that the Spirit of God, who is finally the one who prays from within us to the Father, is also praying through our brother and sister who, in the dryness of the human situation, cannot formulate any prayer.

Those moments of pain and dryness and even bitterness against any idea of God should remind us who are not personally suffering such alienation that we ought not to take prayer too lightly. Prayer is a struggle with God and in that struggle we do not manipulate a God at our disposal but search — often with results that are not apparent -- for a communication in God's own time.

As we go into our own prayer with hope but not assurance of "success", we live side by side with friends who are going through these difficult periods. Our hope is that the God who can accept our sinful and limited prayers will also receive, recognize and console their silence.

For many people, on the other hand, alienation from the church and the Christian faith and the experience of God is the result not of a personal crisis that has shaken their belief but of many years of alienation from Christianity in the sector of society to which they belong.

One sees this, for example, in working-class neighbourhoods in European cities where, for two or three or more generations, labourers have not felt the church at their side in the struggle for justice. So there has taken shape in their life a certain predestination — sociological, not theological — not to believe.

Of course, every human being is not only conditioned by history and family but is also free. This freedom creates the possibility to overcome cultural limitations. Our awareness of sociological trends, tendencies and realities should not therefore blind us to the fact that we are talking about concrete human beings who in their individuality and personality have a chance to respond to a call to faith, personally and individually.

Occasionally in these cases the call of evangelists to repentance and faith in Christ will have a response — not sufficient in number to reverse overall sociological trends but nevertheless providing some individuals the possibility of an experience of faith and a life of prayer.

But if this collective alienation from the church is to give way to a situation in which more than a handful of people are ready to listen to the invitation to faith that will facilitate a life of prayer, a genuine Christian presence is needed, a Christian fermentation that will help to overturn prejudices rooted in the realities of the past. We should be under no illusions about how difficult this will be.

At the same time, those acquainted with the statistics of phenomenal church growth among alienated people in quite a different context — the rapid spread of Pentecostalism among the economically deprived in Latin America — may be inclined to make the cynical charge that this is just a contemporary version of "religion as the opiate of the masses". They will say that the fervent prayers in these services which attract so many people are just a way of diverting their attention from the pain and misery in which they live, and thus serve to prop up an unjust status quo.

Before dismissing this explanation as Marxist rhetoric, we should take an honest and serious look at the evidence. It is undeniable that a real and dangerous component of today's religious scene is the presence of charismatic leaders and organized movements who identify themselves with the Christian faith but have developed sophisticated techniques of manipulating people.

If we talk about Latin America, where much of the fantastic growth of Pentecostal churches has taken place, we are at once reminded of the tragedy in Guyana, when Jim Jones and a group of fanatic believers committed mass suicide in the name of their religious convictions.

Religion is always a very dangerous phenomenon because it has to do with final loyalties, with perceptions of the absolute, with calling to obedience. For that reason we must never lose sight of what we have said several times already: that Jesus Christ must be the criterion of our prayer and that the community which gathers in his name with the open Bible should be the one to judge the manifestation of our religiosity.

At the same time, we do a serious injustice to the Pentecostal movement in Latin America if we consider it only in terms of alienation. We must begin by recognizing that the masses of poor everywhere in the world, but especially in Latin America, are *already* alienated. That means that they are already submitted to the pressures of a society which uses them as cheap human power for industry, which keeps unemployment high in order to keep wages low. They are already being exploited by "populist" leaders, who use them in all sorts of ways that bring them no benefit whatever.

Now within this general alienation of the poor, the Pentecostals are inviting people who are nobody in society to be somebody inside the church. They are called to say Yes or No to God's own invitation. People who have never in their lives been allowed to take a fundamental decision are being told: "You have the key to your own destiny! You can become a child of God!"

In this respect the Pentecostal experience is humanizing and personalizing. And the collective prayer of Pentecostal churches, in which everyone is invited to express himself or herself aloud, creating a tremendous noise, is another way of affirming the immediate value of every person to God and the immediate nearness of God to them in all their aspirations, needs, pain and suffering.

So — granting the possibility for manipulation — we can say that within the total alienation of a whole sector of society, the Pentecostal churches are offering people a chance to be human. As a result, they have produced tremendous consequences at the level of personal and family life.

What they generally lack is an awareness of the social dimension of life: the importance of raising challenges to unjust structures, the need to organize in trade unions and cooperatives and political parties if they are to have a part in shaping society as a whole.

But this is a matter of what has been called conscientization. And here, it seems to me, the Pentecostal churches and the so-called mainline churches must walk together alongside people who have come to recognize themselves as persons but have not gone beyond the transformation of individual and family relationships to wider questions of transformation in society as a whole.

Like all human phenomena, conversion, spirituality and the reality of prayer are ambiguous. We need to recognize the dimensions of alienation present in all popular religiosity. But let us not undervalue the personalizing dimensions present there and the potential generated by reading the Bible and praying together in those communities, discussing together what can be done and discovering together the potential frontiers of action to enter into a fuller participation in the total life of society.

My own country, Uruguay, has traditionally been very secular-minded, with great numbers of people alienated from any religious commitment and identifying themselves as agnostics. Religion was typically viewed as appropriate to women and children, not adults. Yet with the Second Vatican Council, the biblical renewal, the ecumenical movement and theological discussions between Protestants and Catholics focusing on the relevance of the gospel to society, a new attitude in relation to faith has begun to develop. Many who were lukewarm or indifferent to religious experience have become alive to the fact and challenge of Christianity, because they can now see it as relevant to the human situation.

A change in the attitude of the churches towards the problems of society has produced a new attitude towards religious phenomena in individuals in those societies and a new freshness, an opening in relation to religious practices and religious affirmation mediated by the church.

Now the church's solidarity and service must be accompanied by religious faithfulness, a clear liturgical presence, so that people, seeing social involvement and religious discourse, prayer and work, as an integral whole, will consider not only the fruits of the gospel but the gospel itself.

Another serious dimension to this issue is the way urban industrial society frees us from dependence on the cycles of nature. People in rural areas can more easily visualize prayer in relation to the natural phenomena on which their subsistence has traditionally depended. Everything about contemporary urban life, by contrast, seems so organized from morning to night that prayer seems to have no room to influence the chain of events in any significant way.

In our final chapter we will look more closely at the political and social role of prayer in shaping human realities and influencing public opinion.

O Lord, our hearts are heavy
    with the sufferings of the ages,
    with the crusades and the holocausts
    of a thousand thousand years.
The blood of the victims is still warm.
The cries of anguish still fill the night.

To you we lift our outspread hands.
We thirst for you in a thirsty land.

O Lord, who loves us as a father,
    who cares for us as a mother,
    who came to share our life as a brother,
we confess before you
our failure to live as your children,
    brothers and sisters bound together in love.

To you we lift our outspread hands.
We thirst for you in a thirsty land.

We have squandered the gift of life.
The good life of some is built on the pain of many;
the pleasure of a few on the agony of millions.

To you we lift our outspread hands.
We thirst for you in a thirsty land.

We worship death
    in our quest to possess ever more things;
we worship death
    in our hankering after our own security,
    our own survival, our own peace,
as if life were divisible,
as if love were divisible,
as if Christ had not died for all of us.

To you we lift our outspread hands.
We thirst for you in a thirsty land.

O Lord, forgive our life-denying pursuit of life,
and teach us anew what it means to be your children.

To you we lift our outspread hands.
We thirst for you in a thirsty land.

"An act of penitence", from the Worship Book for the WCC's Sixth
Assembly, Vancouver, 1983

5. Prayer and Politics

"Come, Holy Spirit — Renew the Whole Creation"

"Giver of Life — Sustain Your Creation!"
"Spirit of Truth — Set us Free!"
"Spirit of Unity — Reconcile Your People!"
"Holy Spirit — Transform and Sanctify Us!"

The choice of these themes and sub-themes for the Seventh Assembly of the World Council of Churches (scheduled for Canberra, Australia, in early 1991) marks the first time a WCC Assembly theme has taken the form of a prayer.

These prayers grow out of a fundamental recognition that what the church must seek and share with the world today is an awareness of spiritual reality, the realization of an experience of God that can give new vision and power to the whole of humankind.

Throughout these pages we have been speaking of prayer as an opening of human life to God's presence in so intimate a way that we are motivated from within our minds and hearts to enter into the conflicts of history in the spirit of the kingdom of God, in an attempt to be faithful servants of the vision of a world of love and peace, what the Hebrew Bible calls *shalom*.

Prayer is essential and unique, central to Christian life. And prayer for the coming of the Holy Spirit specifically recognizes that we need that intimacy of relation which will give us the courage to go on confronting the vast array of contemporary personal and social conflicts. So when we pray, "Come Holy Spirit, Renew the Whole Creation", we are voicing our belief that an action of God is needed to renew, not only our personal lives but also the entire creation, which is beset by sin manifested in the contamination of the waters, the pollution of the air, the disappearance of animal and vegetable species, the sacking of the whole of nature.

We call on the Spirit of God to come to protect, to renew, to reopen the prospects of life in a world that is becoming so devastated that there is no longer an assurance that coming generations will have a chance to draw sustenance from and enjoy the beauty of nature as we have.

But this is more than a prayer for spiritual power to confront the ecological crisis. It is a cry for help. We appeal to the Spirit to inspire us to enter into the challenges of modern science and technology, to affirm the right of humanity to claim, amidst all the manipulations to which human life is exposed today, the beauty and creativity and freedom and love that belong to God's intent for the whole of creation.

The Assembly sub-themes go on to speak of unity and reconciliation. Make us one, we pray. Help us to be one in the service of the full unity which is your dream for humanity. And they speak of renewal and transformation: the need for sanctification, the aspiration for a life that will show the spirit of Christ in action, the dream of a new heaven and a new earth where the will of God will be implemented.

The prayer to the Holy Spirit is for both the vision of a new world-to-be and the power to participate in the world-that-is — struggling towards that vision of the coming kingdom of God.

The WCC is thus preparing for its Seventh Assembly by a spiritual and intellectual search for resources to transform our personal lives and reshape the life of the church, announcing a new possibility of life for the human community and indeed for the whole cosmos.

This theme and the sub-themes are being used for an Assembly of the World Council of Churches, a once-in-seven-years occasion when representatives of all WCC member churches gather to constitute its highest governing body. In fulfilling this role, the Assembly will assess the programmes and other activities the Council has undertaken over the past seven years and discuss and recommend what it should do in the years ahead.

If the prayers of the theme and subthemes float above the Assembly without any obvious link to the programmatic activities of the WCC, something is seriously wrong. If in the dozens of activities we undertake to fulfill our missionary obedience, to promote ecumenical learning and theological formation, to struggle against racism, to serve the cause of peace, to aid disaster victims, we are not articulating something of the spiritual dimensions of the Bible we read, the liturgy we celebrate and the prayers we raise, we are dangerously close to heresy. The Assembly will be an ideal occasion to stop and rethink what we are doing so that we can attune our activities to the depths of the mystery of God.

I hope that the Assembly's concentration on the vision of the Holy Spirit — whether in biblical and theological reflection on the Spirit's renewal of creation and sanctification of human beings, or in the ongoing quest for church unity against the background of the unity of all humanity, or in the search for discerning the Spirit outside the church in groups working for justice, peace, freedom, reconciliation — will force open our eyes to the reality of the world in such a way that a programme for the WCC (and thus the churches) will be a logical consequence of the encounter between vision and reality.

Prayer is the most down-to-earth exercise human beings can practise. Prayer is encounter with God, to which we bring the concerns of the whole of creation and to which God as Father, as Creator, as Sanctifying Spirit, as motherly Protector, is also bringing his care, his passion, his love for all of created reality.

So this prayer to the Spirit, far from being an escape from reality, brings us back to reality equipped with a deeper vision, a greater commitment and a higher hope.

Political controversy

A perennial source of ecumenical controversy is the fact that this down-to-earth engagement with reality may lead to what is called (often critically) political involvement. To put it in terms of the subject of this book, what is the connection between praying ecumenically for the relief of victims of suffering and injustice and offering diaconal aid or making public declarations and denunciations or supporting with financial and other resources human rights groups and liberation movements?

To these situations of suffering and struggle, the only *unique* contribution Christians and churches bring is a relation to God. In our prayers we call into that struggle the resources drawn from our relation with God. Ecumenically, our contacts with churches and Christian groups may give us access to information that does not often appear in the media, but we do not pretend to have any particular wisdom that is unavailable to others. We do not claim a superior ideology. We share in human historical struggles to overcome known evils.

From the Letter to the Ephesians we draw the insight that these struggles are not first of all against human beings, but against principalities and powers. For such struggles we need protection by "the whole armour of God". We must take on the

Word of God, the spirit of prayer. So when we pray about historical situations or offer diaconal service in areas of human conflict, we call on the deepest resources of our Christian faith.

What we do in praying is to bring to this struggle a dimension of its depth and to appeal to resources that go beyond our human resources to confront powers that are also beyond our human resources. And of course, because our prayer is a Christian prayer, because we pray in the name of Jesus, we must not lose in the heat of our political struggle the dimensions of love, responsibility and care for human beings that characterized Jesus' attitude.

There is a built-in paradox here. On the one hand, we bring to our engagement in a conflict situation this dimension of its religious, spiritual, eschatological significance — almost, one could say, a "crusading" spirit. On the other hand, while not detracting from the seriousness of the struggle, because we bring our prayer in the name of Jesus and hold the model of his life and teaching before us, we assess it as finally being submitted to a higher judgment than ours.

So poor Christians in Latin America who rally around the cause of justice by marching in a religious procession or celebrating a worship service before risking an encounter with the police are not only calling God to their side. They are also saying, "You who are the highest Judge, judge and purify us too."

A Marxist leader in the German Democratic Republic once told me, "You Christians will never lead a revolution, because before you reach the moment of decision you take so much time coming to terms with your holy God in heaven that the opportunity for action passes you by."

"Maybe you're right," I told him. "Perhaps we will hesitate for a moment longer than the others. But it is precisely because we take that moment to place our historical endeavours under God's scrutiny that we can contribute the dimension of humanity and personal care which should never be absent from even the greatest historical struggles."

Often, of course, it is concrete cases rather than general principles over which disputes arise among Christians in the ecumenical movement. Again I refer to the example of South Africa. Some WCC member churches have objected to our distribution of liturgical materials that have included prayers for the overthrow of the white minority government which oppresses the black majority there. Many of those who register such objections would not in any way defend the unjust system of apartheid. But they suggest that rather than praying for those in power to be overthrown, we should pray that they will repent of their unjust deeds. In other words, we should be praying for their conversion.

Our prayers about South Africa will in the first place arise out of our care for the victims of that situation. And it is clear that among the victims are the Afrikaner establishment, the National Party and the State President himself. Of course, just as I know that, as a sinner before God, I can live from day to day only on the basis of the forgiveness of my sins, I will also consider the South African State President to be a sinner, called, just as I am, to repentance. Thus a dimension of judgment is implicit in any of our prayers about a particular government or person or situation. As we said above, we are appealing to the higher judgment of God.

But the final aim for which we are praying is the coming of the kingdom of God. And the aim of the kingdom of God is the triumph of love. In our prayers we dare to dream that the leaders of the National Party can be called to repent and to create new opportunities for themselves and their people by coming into the sight of the forces of the kingdom.

At the same time as we express Christian concern for fellow-sinners who are responsible for the continuation of repressive situations, we also pray for the removal of tyrannical governments, for that, too, includes the potential of salvation and liberation for the members of that government. Once a person is deprived of power, he or she is freed from a serious temptation and given a new chance to analyze his or her life and the lives that depend on it.

When we do come to the point of praying for the removal of a particular government or for radical changes in a particular unjust social structure, we are praying for the elimination of factors of oppression which are so obviously contrary to the will of God that they cannot be tolerated.

When Jesus came into the temple and overturned the tables of the merchants doing business there, he was obviously calling them to repent by making a dramatic point of their sinful behaviour. At the same time, he was symbolically and physically making the affirmation that the house of God is a house of prayer, not a den of thieves.

His action was also motivated by compassion for the pilgrims who had been exploited in that temple and for the humble worshippers who were being deprived of a chance to engage in that for which the temple had been built. His concern for the merchants came to expression through an upheaval of the evil structures they had built and in which they were imprisoned. So, too, when we pray for South Africa, we are praying for all of the protagonists in that situation. But we are also praying for an opening of that situation in the direction of the kingdom of God.

Sometimes our recognition of the spiritual dimension of the struggles around us may tempt Christians to overlook the political complexities of the situations about which we pray. We must remember that we are not just Christians; we are also normal human beings, who share with others the analysis of society. There is a sober realism in the biblical testimony — for instance, Jesus invites us to consider the strength of our enemies — which warns us to be cautious in any historical and political involvements.

But within the process of thinking, planning and organizing that goes into analyzing a situation and strategizing about appropriate tactics, we bring the dimension of eternity, hoping that placing it in the perspective of the kingdom will give meaning to the whole enterprise. It is at this point that we add the power of commitment to the struggle and the restraint of those who know that we are all under the higher judgment of God and in need of forgiveness for our sins.

So we are not saying that our only contribution is to pray. We are saying that the contribution that only Christians can offer is this reminder of the deepest meaning of the historical situation and the highest level of hope to which we are being called.

We pray and we work. But some will say that within the ecumenical movement we tend to pray and work only about some areas of conflict in the world, while largely ignoring vast areas of injustice and suffering.

This is of course true. We cannot help being selective in view of the limits of our human resources and wisdom. We can embrace the whole, for instance, in our liturgical prayers for nature, for good harvests in the whole world, for those who travel on sea and by air. We make prayers of a general nature that embrace the wholeness of the creation, and we need to keep those prayers alive. But we are unable to embrace the whole existentially.

The moment our prayers become linked to concrete historical situations, we obviously bring to God's attention those sectors of humanity which in a given moment touch our community the most deeply or closely. Aware that we are not the only sector of the Christian community to be praying, we hope that God will listen to our prayers not only in their concrete historical, social and geographical reference but also as symbolic of priestly intercession for all similar situations.

This selectivity is evident in the liturgical prayers of many traditions: to pray for patriarchs and bishops is to pray for the whole church; to pray for queens and presidents is to pray for the whole nation they represent or govern. Although there is no escape from such selectivity, we must be humble enough to be corrected and to learn from others who are asking for our prayer.

In the case of the World Council of Churches, this charge of selectivity usually takes the form of faulting our indignation against the sins of the nations of the Western world compared with our relative silence about the sins of the Eastern socialist nations.

I think we have been interceding — and will continue to intercede — without taking an ideological stance but in actual reference to what is going on. Recently, for example, we have raised many prayers ecumenically in relation to the ethnic strife in Soviet Armenia. We prayed for peace and reconciliation in Afghanistan, which involved, of course, prayer for the withdrawal of Soviet troops and other external influences there. But in the final analysis it is true that there is selectiveness in our prayer, and that is unavoidable given the concreteness of our prayers as well as particular factors in the situations about which we pray.

We must also honestly admit that when we make our ecumenical confession of sins, there is a great temptation to place the emphasis on other people's sins rather than our own. This of course is not a peculiarly ecumenical failing. It is present in all the saints in the history of the church and it is present today in the prayers of every Christian and every church.

But let us be careful. To be sure, we are all sinners. To say that is to utter a theological truth. But there is something wrong with our theology if it makes no distinction between the sadistic frenzy of the torturer and the hatred of the prisoner being tortured. In God's eyes, not every sinful attitude has the same dimensions. There are people — the poor, the racially oppressed, women, children — who are in a special way *sinned against*. Aware of their suffering from the structural, collective sins of others, we may, in solidarity, make a confession that denounces the sins of their oppressors. Of course, we should not ignore our own complicity in the sins we are denouncing.

We must avoid making religious judgments in a way that eliminates any possibility of making historical judgments. To understand the cherished doctrine of the justification of the sinner by faith through grace as implying that everyone is equally justified without the expressions of repentance we see in Zacchaeus, without the challenge to the wealthy young man whom Jesus urged to sell all his worldly goods, is to use theology to sacralize the status quo and mock the gospel of justice, the good news preached to the poor.

So it is not only the ecumenical movement that has a tendency to highlight the sins of others. All of us are permanently under that temptation. The only protection against it is first of all to confess *our* sins and to acknowledge before God how little we are doing of what we could be doing. There is a danger of pharisaism in our ecumenical prayers. But there is a danger of escapism in many prayers that seek to view cases of conflict and human suffering in such completely theological terms as to ignore the power-realities of the situation.

Politics and unity

Since ecumenism is primarily a movement for the unity of the church, it is evident that bringing political situations into our prayers may be troublesome. Far from moving us towards Christian unity, the inclusion of concretely "political" petitions in our prayers may tend to break community, particularly if it seems to bring with it the insinuation that those who disagree with the political analysis behind the petition are placing themselves outside of Christian fellowship.

The theme of the WCC's Fifth Assembly (Nairobi, 1975) — "Jesus Christ frees and unites" — came to life out of just such a tension. While some people accent the liberation brought by Jesus Christ and the corresponding freedom that should characterize human life, others place more emphasis on unity and breaking down barriers as the main target of the ecumenical movement.

The former may be inclined to urge ecumenical engagement wherever people are in bondage, taking an unambiguous political stand against repressive forces even if some within the ecumenical community are uncomfortable with such a stand or indeed refuse to associate themselves with it. The latter may insist on allowing the community to be as wide as possible, drawing only those lines which are absolutely necessary to keep the fellowship from falling into overt self-contradiction, even if this sometimes means blunting the edge of the ecumenical political witness.

There is a permanent tension here, one which is by no means limited to the ecumenical movement. In some contexts it may take the form of an argument between those who urge a "prophetic" stance and those who call for a "priestly" role. It will often surface in disagreement between members or groups within a single denomination or even at the parish or congregational level.

Wisely, I think, the World Council of Churches has struggled to keep those two dimensions together. Unity is of course central to our ecumenical life because it belongs to the heart of Jesus' prayer and the Father's will. But that unity is in the service of mission "so that the world may believe". And the world will be able to believe only if it looks to Jesus Christ and can, through the wounded side and the pierced hands, discern the cross.

This means that there is no way we can call people to unity unless we show that it in the spirit of what God was doing in the cross of Jesus Christ, which was the consequence of his taking sides with the downtrodden, the marginal, the powerless. There *is* a risk in political prayer; there is more than a risk, there is an inevitability of conflict.

Let us, however, look at prayer and politics in the light of the historical record. The majority of the prayers in the Bible are of a political nature. From the songs of the book of Judges through the Psalms, through the prophets, through the life of Jesus as recorded in the gospels, there is a historical dimension to what is being prayed for.

Consider, for example, Jesus' very "spiritual" sounding prayer: "I thank thee, Father, Lord of heaven and earth, that thou hast hidden these things from the wise and understanding and revealed them to babes" (Matthew 11:25). He was referring here to a concrete historical experience. The powerful of his day were rejecting his invitation and plotting to murder him. Soldiers were being sent after him. And he saw that those who were listening were the poor, who had no significance in the life of the people. It was they who were given the gift to understand and were following him. So it is a spiritual expression — "I thank you that this kingdom is passing through the poor" — but it is also a prayer that cannot be understood apart from a real political confrontation.

Or consider Gethsemane, where Jesus prayed, "O Lord, if it is possible let this cup pass from me!". The "cup" to which he was referring was a real political confrontation within history. Already the powers of darkness had negotiated his betrayal with one of his own disciples. The soldiers were on the way to the garden. The horror of death on the cross was on the horizon. Jesus could have escaped. He could have taken another political option. But in the strength of this prayer, he accepted the will of his Father to go through the suffering of the cross for our salvation, our liberation.

The history of the church may not disclose such admirable examples as the Bible (though there are some not-so-admirable partisan prayers in Scripture as well, and we should not unfairly judge the more recent history of the church just because we have much more information about it).

Think, for example, of the chaplains in the armies of the world. They are not employed by the military only to keep soldiers thinking of the glories of heaven before they go into battle. Throughout the history of the so-called Christian nations of Europe, all kinds of prayers have blessed armies or this or that national policy.

One need only recall the polemics that broke out in Great Britain after the end of the Falklands-Malvinas war. The government wanted the Church of England to offer a thanksgiving celebration for the military victory. Instead, the Archbishop of Canterbury organized a service of intercession for all those who suffered in the war, calling for reconciliation among the peoples. On the one side was the classic attitude of a powerful nation asking the church to bless its endeavours without introducing the critical dimension that is essential to Christian prayer. On the other side was a faithful church *assuming* a political role, bringing into prayer the realities of a world of hate and war but not accepting the reduction of those prayers to the service of a party line.

One can also point to a negative link between prayer and politics in those Christian movements which concentrate so much on celebrating their own religious experience that they invite people to forget what is going on in daily life — not recognizing how this helps to maintain the dominance of what may be an unjust status quo.

Whether by action or abstention, Christians are always immersed in the world of human co-responsibility which we call politics. Prayer and concern for the *polis,* concern for human beings, are always together.

Ecumenically, the Falklands-Malvinas conflict is instructive. While actual hostilities were going on between Argentina and the United Kingdom, the content of our ecumenical prayer was relatively straightforward: a petition for an end to the killing and destruction and for the protection of all those who were in battle. But once the conflict ended with the issue left unresolved, what kind of prayers could we offer ecumenically?

At the international level, the answer seems again to be relatively straightforward. We intercede for the opening of hearts to understand each other. We pray for dialogue, for reconciliation, for avoidance of recourse to military action, for elimination of mutual hatred. But even this apparent "neutrality" on the issue *per se* is complicated. For in our prayer that the two sides would come to the negotiating table, we were already taking sides with those who said we must negotiate everything, as against those who were saying that the issue of the sovereignty of the islands was not up for negotiation.

But the ecumenical community is more than its central expression in the World Council of Churches. It also includes the churches of Argentina and the churches of Great Britain. They, too, are praying; and as they pray, they are almost unavoidably raising their own particular perspectives and biases.

In this example, of course, my personal sympathy as a Latin American is close to the position taken by Argentina. But that is a secondary matter. The important thing is that ecumenically we need to keep our brothers and sisters in both Argentina and Great Britain aware that other brothers and sisters, equally honest in their relationship to God and their aspiration for the coming of his kingdom, have different perspectives on this situation.

If we do that, there is a chance that we can develop an honest dialogue — and the WCC has, in this situation and others, mediated such encounters between Christians in different national situations. Our hope is that this may somehow help to pave the way for the kind of negotiations that will at some point lead to a solution. We need to do all we can to keep the inevitable tension between the two members of the body creative.

Prayer is the opening of our total life before God in an attempt to gain access not only to God's resources, but also to the purifying fire of God's judgment and correction of our own stance. By bearing this in mind we acknowledge the seriousness of our situation and indicate that in God's wisdom solutions to our historical dilemmas must be sought. We cannot simply wash our hands and accommodate ourselves to the prevailing situation.

Praying and disagreeing

Not everyone will be satisfied with this. Some will object to praying about a given situation alongside those with whom they disagree completely.

Sometimes this objection arises at the theological level. Doctrinally conservative Christians may say that they consider it wrong to engage in so solemn an exercise as prayer with those who hold sharply different views on what they see as the fundamentals of the faith. We ought not, they say, to pray with heretics.

At the intellectual level this objection is fairly easy to answer within the context of the WCC. The Basis of the Council includes a number of theological affirmations with which all member churches express their agreement: trinitarian faith in God the Father, Son and Holy Spirit, confession of Jesus Christ as God and Saviour, a commitment to work together in his name in the world together.

Furthermore, the experience of life together in the ecumenical movement has led to broad ecumenical convergence — even if it does not yet take shape in credal affirmations — on a number of other issues: the incompatibility of racism with Christian faith, the poor as the criteria for the genuineness of our witness in the world and so on.

So one could say, from the perspective of the WCC, that all those who confess Jesus Christ as God and Saviour, all those who worship God as the Trinity, are entitled to pray together — and indeed find it easy to pray together — because they express in the same words and symbols the vision of God to whom our prayers are being addressed. We pray together with all who confess God the Father, Son and Holy Spirit in such a way as to make it evident that we are addressing the same vision, conception, likeness of God.

We must also recognize that there are Christians whose sincerity and spirituality we cannot doubt — because the fruits of devotion and love are in them — who do not express their faith in terms exactly compatible with the Basis of the WCC. If we express our theological presuppositions differently, we may obviously have difficulties praying together. Perhaps the most we can do in these cases is to keep silence or to read the Psalms together.

Yet even if we find the doctrinal freedom to pray together, there remains the question of praying with those with whom we have sharp differences on ethical questions.

The Basis of the WCC is a yardstick that helps me in coming together to pray with other Christians. I reserve an existential freedom of the Spirit to bring me together in prayer with people who do not articulate their fundamental beliefs in exactly in the same categories but show other indications that we share a common object of our faith. I would use a similar argument in relation to ethical disagreements among Christians.

It is obvious that as we go into the areas of Christian obedience in problems of justice and peace, Christians do not always agree. Sometimes, indeed, the disagreements are so sharp that in a war Christians kill each other. Could we pray together in those circumstances?

The fundamental criteria for the "reciprocal recognition" needed to come together in prayer are love of God and love of neighbour, acknowledgement of the equality of all children of God in Christ and giving of preference to the poor. Within these criteria, I am free to pray with someone whose political solutions are so different from mine that he or she feels obliged to combat my options. In other words, I can pray with anyone who, in my judgment, is willing to try to justify what he or she is doing along the lines of a gospel commitment to love of neighbour, the equality of all human beings and the priority to the poor.

Where there are attitudes that I cannot reconcile with those things, of course praying together is very difficult. Even so, prayer together could be a way to open up the correction of the Spirit, or to bring a higher perspective for judging between or among us and perhaps to produce some breakthrough into a new dimension of reality where our contradictions could find a solution.

At the same time, I need to reserve an area of freedom for the Spirit in this connection, too, in order to avoid the pharisaism of supposing that I am right and the other is totally wrong.

In a recent meeting of the WCC Central Committee, a resolution was passed calling the churches to support the international boycott on an oil company operating in South Africa. I know that many persons in the leadership of that oil company are faithful Christians. Many of them believe that their actions in South Africa are undermining apartheid.

So we disagree at the level of strategy. We need to be sure that we do not disagree at the level of solidarity with the people of South Africa and rejection of the evil of apartheid in its totality. Prayer together might give us a chance to discuss the seriousness of the situation and to challenge each other to do the kind of action that is necessary.

So, while I follow the Central Committee in its radical decision and invite other Christians to support that decision, I recognize that there are some Christians who have difficulties in following this. By praying together we avoid pharisaical ideas of superiority over others, without of course eliminating the actual political conflict, which still needs to be confronted.

Of course, we must be aware of the possibility that by praying together with persons with whom we have ethical disagreements we may lend a certain credibility to their position. Praying together is not only a purely religious act of projecting our lives into God. It is also a social act. If I, as general secretary of the World Council of Churches, worship together with leaders of transnational corporations, I give some credentials to them (and, from their point of view, they are likely giving some credentials to me, given the image of the WCC in some of these circles).

Thus we must be spiritually and politically responsible when coming to pray together. But in any case, at the risk of those misunderstandings, I do not think we can refuse to expose ourselves together in front of God to the correction of God.

The limits to this are set by what has, in classical doctrinal terminology, been called the *anathema:* the moment in which the church considers some person or some body as completely outsdie the realm of the Christian faith. In the past such declarations were often made in connection with doctrinal positions; today, we are more inclined to come to this point in ethical questions. In the case of apartheid, several church and ecumenical bodies have declared that the denial of apartheid belongs to our confession of Jesus Christ, our status as Christians.

Thus, the possibility of praying together is removed when it comes to those who consciously support and defend the apartheid system. At that moment, we consider that there is a breaking of relation with God that makes it impossible, without clear repentance, to be able to come together in prayer before God.

But it is different in those other situations, which are by far the majority, where disputes centre on methodologies and tactics, where we may suspect that fear or self-interest has coloured a person's political stance. In the ambiguity of all human situations, we must be willing to enter into the ecumenical discipline of listening to each other in search for a better and more intelligent obedience.

Since our worship and prayer are never matters of our own merit, but always something that calls on the Spirit and grace of God, we should be very careful not to discriminate too quickly about who can participate in this communion of the family of God.